Herbert Warington Smyth

Notes of a Journey on the Upper Mekong, Siam

With Maps and Illustrations

Herbert Warington Smyth

Notes of a Journey on the Upper Mekong, Siam
With Maps and Illustrations

ISBN/EAN: 9783744798433

Printed in Europe, USA, Canada, Australia, Japan

Cover: Foto ©Andreas Hilbeck / pixelio.de

More available books at **www.hansebooks.com**

NOTES OF

A JOURNEY ON THE UPPER MEKONG, SIAM.

BY

H. WARINGTON SMYTH,

OF THE ROYAL DEPARTMENT OF MINES AND GEOLOGY, BANGKOK.

WITH MAPS AND ILLUSTRATIONS.

PUBLISHED FOR

THE ROYAL GEOGRAPHICAL SOCIETY

BY

JOHN MURRAY, 50, ALBEMARLE STREET, LONDON.
1895.

THE RAPIDS AT THE GATES OF CHIENG KONG, MEKONG RIVER.

PREFACE.

I HAVE put together the following account of a recent journey made
for the Siamese Government to the Mekong valley, chiefly for the
reason that at the present moment, when the French have "rectified"
their boundaries on the north and east of Siam to the extent of some
85,000 square miles, more interest than usual will probably be felt
in the character of the country and the people, of whom there are
not too many reliable accounts to be found. At the same time,
I feel very strongly that there are others whose descriptions will
be far more valuable than my own, owing to their longer residence
in the country, and the greater extent of their explorations.
I refer especially to Messrs. McCarthy, Archer, and Beckett, who
have done difficult and extensive work in all parts of Siam and
the Laos states; and there is certainly no European, and probably no
Siamese, that knows so much of the configuration of the north-east
as does Mr. McCarthy, who, carried on by an apparently deep love of
jungle-life, has aroused the admiration of the Siamese and Laos at
Luang Prabang by his hardihood and energy, and the results of
whose work were a constant source of admiration to me, as I went
on and saw the wildness and difficulty of the country.

The object of my journey was primarily the examination, for the
Siamese Government, of a supposed very rich deposit of gems (rubies
and sapphires), lately discovered on the left bank of the Mekong,
opposite Chieng Kong. My orders were to return by Luang Prabang,
Nongkhai, and Khorat, and to visit and report on all mineral
deposits of which I could get information, gathering all geological

data which were possible. The time allowed was six months, and I was not to leave the general line of march prescribed by more than 60 miles. I need hardly say—and every one who knows what jungle-travelling is will understand—that my programme, to be thoroughly carried through over the large extent of country marked out, might well occupy six years instead of months; and that such a hurried exploration in a country covered densely with forest—which, next perhaps to snow, is the greatest enemy to the science of geology —could not but be unsatisfactory to one's self.

H. WARINGTON SMYTH.

GLOSSARY.

Pak = mouth of a river; *e.g.* Pak Oo, mouth of river Oo.
Nam = river; *e.g.* Nam Oo, river Oo (*a* always long, as in *barn*).
Hoay = mountain torrent.
Keng = rapid; *e.g.* Keng Fapa, Fapa rapid.
Luaug = great or chief; *e.g.* Keng Luang, the great rapid.
Doi *or* puh = Siam word Kao = hill.
Ban *or* Bang = house or village (used indiscriminately).
Sala = rest-house.
Muang = town or township, often district or province.
Chow Muang = literally, chief of the township = governor.
K'loug = stream or canal.

CONTENTS.

MAPS AND ILLUSTRATIONS.

—◆◇◆—

NOTES OF

Á JOURNEY ON THE UPPER MEKONG, SIAM.

PART I.

BANGKOK TO MUANG NAN.

EARLY in December, 1892, we left Bangkok—myself, three Siamese assistants, and a sergeant's guard as escort, and coolies. At Muang Chainat, owing to the rapid fall of the river, I had to send back the Navy launch, which was drawing 3 feet 6 inches; a month earlier she might have got nearly up to M.* Pechai. At Paknam Pho, where the Nam Pho and Meiping meet, after a good deal of bargaining I secured a *rua nua*, or uorth-land boat, to take me on. Boat-travelling in Siam is much the same everywhere; and in their boat-life, it may be said, the Siamese have attained a high degree of civilization. Very often the boat is the home of the family, and after the rains they moor alongside the bank and cultivate tobacco, cotton, or melons on the slope on which the rich loam of the floods has settled down; after the rice harvest they will set out laden with paddy for Bangkok, returning later on with salt or other luxuries from the south. The Chinese, who are the most energetic people in the country, carry on extensive trading in this way. They use a very large double-ended kind of boat, known as "rice-boat,"

---

* M. = Muaug.

which has a long cylindrical roof of closely plaited work impervious to rain, extending from just before the helmsman to within 10 feet of the bows, where the two or three oarsmen toil at the long oars. As in all the Siamese boats, the oar is slung in a grommet, which is turned round the top of a small pole firmly let into the gunwale at the lower end. This gives the end of the oar sufficient height inboard,

THE MEINAM BELOW CHAINAT.

and the oarsman stands to his work facing forward, the outer hand on a small handle turned at right angles to the oar, as in the Chinese sampans one sees in the straits. With a big heavy boat, the action, with a sharp jerk at the end of the stroke, is not pretty; but in the small *rua chang* (or sampan) of the city the motion is exactly

LOADED RICE-BOATS LYING IN BANGKOK.

that of the gondolier, and with the swaying motion of the inside leg, which is often quite free, is extremely pretty. It must be confessed the grommet principle, which at least keeps the oar in its place, makes the work much easier than the slippery crutch in which the gondolier at Venice works his long oar, and which proves a great source of difficulty to the beginner in the art. This method is known by the Siamese as " chaw "- (or " chow "-) ing.

Next in size and usefulness to the "rice-boats" (which are

generally about 40 feet long, 10 feet 4 inches beam, with 6 feet 4 inches extreme draught when loaded, and carry twenty koyans of rice) comes the *rua pet*, which is a great favourite with the Siamese.

It is cleaner lined than the rice-boat, the cabin arrangement being the same; that is, the long roof, the deck at the level of the gunwale going fore and aft, and the storage-room all be-

RUA PET.

low, reached by taking out the neatly fitting pieces of deck, which are made to fit into the main cross-beams. The helmsman has a slightly raised attap roof over his head, and he (or she, for the wife and the children down to six years old can steer as well as the father) looks out from under this and over the long low roof in front. The steering is done with a rudder shipped in the usual way on the stern-post, while in the big rice-boat it is generally on the quarter (if under sail, on the lee quarter), kept in position by a rope grommet at the head, and another lanyard put through an eye bored lower down. In both kinds of craft a finely peaked calico lugsail is used with a fair wind—the matting, of which the junks and local coast-luggers make their sails, being never seen inland. The size of the *rua pet* is generally 40 feet over all, 8 feet 4 inches beam, and 3 feet 4 inches draught loaded; a new one will cost 300 to 320 ticals, say £26. Teak is largely used in the construction, and when finished the whole is covered with a coating of *chunam*, a mixture of oil from the Mai Yang (a magnificently proportioned tree common in the forest), with dammar oil, which gives a beautiful red varnish to the hull.

A third distinct type of boat is the *rua nua* ("nua" meaning north, and "rua" boat), which seems to be rather a Laos than a Siamese form. It is hardly accurate to call them distinctively "Laos boats," as is often done, as the real "Laos boat," used both on the Mekong and in the Laos states proper on the Meinam, is simply a long dug-out canoe, 60 feet long, with an extreme beam of 4 feet. The *rua nua* is a much more highly developed type, and is in construction as elaborate as those above mentioned. It is generally longer than the *rua pet*. My boat was 56 feet 10 inches over all,

with a beam of 10 feet, and carried the owner and his crew of
four men, with myself and twenty Siamese. At night a few of us
slept on shore, in the Salas or rest-houses of the monasteries, or on
the banks of sand. The stem and stern posts are made of huge
chocks of teak, the bottom flat of three or four huge planks running
the whole length of the boat if possible. Right aft is a high-roofed

RUA NUA.

and very comfortable house in which the steersman lives; sitting
on his high stool, and looking over the usual plaited roof along the
centre of the boat, he turns his long steering-oar, which reaches far
out astern over the port quarter. The fore-deck of the boat is out-
rigged on each side to a considerable distance, while a gangway runs
round the centre roof outside for the man to pole along. Up the
Meiping these boats are generally ornamented with a long high snout
of timber out forward, and a high forked tail astern.

Of small craft the variety is endless—from the small canoes
which hawk *kanoms*, or cakes of rice, sugar, and coconut, to the small
roughly roofed boats which will just hold the owner and his wife
and child if they balance carefully, or the long snake-like boats which
are favourites with the monks at the monasteries. The people usually
build their own boats, and are very good hands at it; and one may
see them in all states of construction,—hollowed out with laborious
chipping ready for opening out over the fire, or already heated
and opened up, with knees and ribs being put in and pegged with
wood (for, like the Norwegians, they never use nails, and the result
is great durability); or ready with a six-inch "wash-streak" all
round, and the light deck at the gunwale level, which is the feature
of the smallest, if we except the *sampans* and canoes of the capital.

The fittings of the large species of craft above described are often elaborate and almost yacht-like. A brass trimming to the gunwale, and bright red prayer-papers, are generally to be seen on board of John Chinaman. There will be pretty balustrades round the quarters where the helmsman is, partly for show, partly to keep the small fry from falling overboard. Curtains of plaited bamboo are hinged to the attap roof above the helmsman, and when shut down will keep out rain or sun. At the fore end the deck will shine

RUA NUA FROM FORE END.

with the polish given it by the constant sitting or reclining of the crew, and inside the long low roof, if there were only sufficient head-room, the floor would be declared perfect for a dance. All round are lockers, in which cotton stuffs are stored to take up-country,

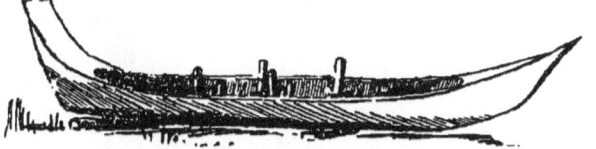

BOAT HOLLOWED OUT OF TRUNK READY TO BE SOAKED IN RIVER.

BOAT OPENED OUT OVER FIRE, RIBS AND KNEES IN.

or betel-box, teapot, and crockery are stowed; the comfort and luxury of some of these boats could not be surpassed.

And how they do all enjoy life! There is no hurry; if going down stream, they take it easy enough; and if going up, why over-work? A week earlier or a week later makes no difference; and so, why not stop and have some tea and chat as they pass some friendly village, or a boat with whom last year perhaps they travelled in company for a month? If the sun gets hot, they will tie up to the bank, and all hands bathe, the children diving overboard like the best of them. If it rains, tie up again, light up the fire and cook the rice and mix the curry for supper; then out cigarettes all hands, and from the cloud, to which even the stout five-year-old boy, who is the pet of the ship, contributes his share, gaze complacently out into the

RICE-BOATS AND FLOATING HOUSE, PAKNAM PHO.

damp evening, where all the myriad life of jungle is piping shrilly in the swaying bamboo clumps. No wonder these people are happy and hospitable, ever ready with a joke.

The journey to Muang Pechai took our *rua nua* 19 days, and owing to the falling state of the river, our old skipper had to lighten

A RICE-BOAT, FLYING LIGHT.

his ship by selling off a lot of his salt; and even then she drew 3 feet, and all hands had frequently to go overboard and haul over shallows.

Above the junction of the Meinam Yome and the Pechai River, the villages which had thronged the bank gave way to a wild uninhabited country—the villages few and poor, the paddy-fields far apart and small. The river winds tortuously between clay banks 30 feet high and crowned with the prickly bamboo or long grasses, or in places with deep forests of fine timber. Here and there on the inside of the bend would be extensive sandbanks, and on these, as being safer from wild animals or fever, often three or four boats' crews would be camping at night. On the concave side of the bend would be evidences of huge falls of stuff, the result of the recent floods, with large trees or bamboo clumps sticking out of the water. Of animal life there was plenty—the apparently sluggish crocodile, which at the crack of a rifle would leap his own length into the water; the familiar and friendly long-tailed monkeys; or the white-headed fish-eagle, and another big dark-coloured eagle with peculiarly hoarse cry.

The order Herodiones is well represented, and I shot specimens of the common heron (*Ardea cinerea*), and the great white heron or

RICE RAFT, NAM OO.

great egret (*Ardea alba*); and in the low state of one's larder, which is the normal condition in Siam, they were excellent eating. Of kingfishers I saw two distinct forms—the smaller one (?), the pied kingfisher of India; the larger with a stronger bill, black and white, without the high colouring of the other. All these birds are very common, and there are many smaller thin-legged birds running along the sands.

As in all the rivers of Siam during and just after the rains, the water is alive with fish, the most remarkable that I saw being the " pla reum," a creature often over 3 feet long and the same in depth— very broad-bodied, with a covering of large scales, the fins, tail, and gills of a pinky red; head large and broad, with wide mouth lined with fine rows of diminutive teeth, of which there are two lines in the upper jaw. The tail is enormously powerful in the water, and, until he is tired out, the drift-net used for catching him has a very hard time of it.

After reaching Muang Pichit, the villages occur more frequently again, and are often palisaded; this is necessary for the protection of the cattle, which are the favourite prey of the dacoits who wander about in the valley of the Meinam all too freely, often with fine boats, which in the daytime are peaceful trading craft to the eye, but at night suddenly bristle with men. At the present time this kind of business is an actual danger to the traders as well as to the peaceful villagers; and at the time I went up, though the Minister of the North (Prince Damrong) had just been on a tour to Pechai, they were extremely bold all over the country. Once north of lat. 17° 40', and in the Laos country, property is safer than in Eaton Square.

One word as to the "wats," or monasteries, and the monks who inhabit them. They are often misnamed "temples" and "priests;" but, as all who know the customs of the Buddhist countries around will be aware, there is no "priesthood" proper. These men are really retired from the world for the purpose of such meditation as shall bring them as near to the purity of their master and pattern Buddha as possible. Wherever there are villages there are wats, supported by the contributions of the inhabitants, who are bent on gaining merit by their good deeds to these holy men. Like the monks of "merrie England" in years gone by, there are good, bad, and indifferent; in many cases the prior is a keen Pâli student and good musician, and a man of some ideas. The yellow robe and the shaving of head and eyebrows is not exactly fascinating at a close view, but among the monks I used. to see many very fine thoughtful faces; while I shall, I hope, always remember the friendly evenings I spent after the day's voyage, sitting perched on the bamboo flooring of the sala, high above the quiet stream, listening to a duet played on their simple two-stringed fiddles. The body is made of half a coconut-shell, over which the sounding-board is placed. The string of the bow is between the two strings, and the execution is wonderful. The airs, which are all handed down by ear, are a very fast weird music, distinctly catchy, and one, "the trotting pony," is a wonderfully sweet and descriptive air. Another instrument is the *toka*, a hollow teak sounding-box with two strings stretched over a number of bridges, on which the fingers of the left hand work while the right twangs the strings: this joined in very well with the fiddles. The intervals are not the same as ours, and the European ear takes some time to get accustomed to the novelty; after a time, however, one can sufficiently interpret the airs to get them on a flute, whereon the proper intervals seem to enable one to get a correct version of what before seemed rather a jargon. Another favourite pursuit with the youthful monks is *tetakvoa*, a football of open wicker-work, which is kept going by the dozen or so players taking "full volleys" with knee or foot, and often "heading" the ball. This, of course, is common in the villages too, but I did not see it in the Laos states.

It 'is the custom to bring up for the night, whenever possible, alongside one of these wats, both on account of the convenience of finding a good sala, and the greater security against robbers. There is always a wide clear space beneath the trees which shade the buildings of the monastery, and some of these quiet spots, from which, as one walks up and down in the evening, one sees the long reach of river reflecting the last light in the west, or, in the chilly morning, the first streaks of dawn, are almost ideal places for retirement and meditation. They, and the life which goes on within, have been admirably described by Shway Yoe, in his book 'The Burman,' one of the completest pictures which has ever been drawn of any people; and the monastery life of Siam is almost identical. As the monotonous but almost weird chant of the monks floated out across the stream at sunset, we used to tie up for the night beneath: often it would go far on into the night; and then long before day the great gong would begin its clanging, and once more the chant rise among the mists, and for us another day's poling would commence.

In the Laos states there are many points of difference in the wats, not only in the architecture (and the hill-wats become very simple, with a few roughly baked bricks for the low walls, and a thatch roof in place of the red or wood tiled roofs of Siam), but also in the *régime*. Every boy, for instance, who goes to do his schooling at the wat wears the yellow robe, which assumes thus almost the character of the college gown at home, and until he has so worn it he has no title to the name of "man." As in Siam, besides his letters, he learns the elementary precepts taught by Buddha; but, as not in Siam, he often goes out with his superiors into the jungle, with robe tucked up, to hew wood or do other work for the support of the wat, which the laymen, being too few or too poor, cannot do.

During this month of December the north-east monsoon was blowing, but we had curiously cloudy cool days nearly all the time, with, at the start, slight rain at times.   The minimum reading of the thermometer was 42° Fahr. on the 22nd, just before sunrise.   The two following mornings we had 45° Fahr.; the maxima in the shade of the steersman's house being 73°, 77,° and 76° on those days. 50°, 52·5°, 49°, 51°, 54°, 57°, 50°, and 57° were the minima for the next eight days, and the maximum recorded was 85° at 1 p.m.   At 9 a.m. the thermometer was never above 64°.

At Muang Fitsanulok, which stands along a very pretty sweep of water, hid deep in its areca and banana palms, I spent a morning at wat Chinareth.   This was the nearest approach to a real piece of effective architecture that I had seen since leaving, and I once more experienced the feeling of exultation which one used to know at home, when enjoying the lights and shadows of some old building where the mind of man had worked with great result.   An additional charm was the colouring.   The coloured tiles of the roofs of the wats are remarkable in Bangkok; but far in the jungle, when the eye has become accustomed to green for weeks, the wonderful yellow-red, picked off with green borders, and the light-red lower buildings of the cloisters, were most striking.   The building was once very extensive, cruciform in shape, in four distinct sections round the great central tower.   The western building is the only one in any sort of preservation, and south of it, and at its south-western end, still stand the cloisters.   Brick and laterite blocks are the material used, the former in some cases, as in the wall and the pillars of the cloister, being stuccoed.   These little pillars are only 6 feet high, and the roof is gabled, supported on simple uprights, which rise from horizontal cross-beams resting on the pillars; and so a very pretty and simple cloister walk is obtained.   The remains of such walks lie in every direction round the centre.   As for the western building itself, I was much delighted with the interior.   One enters a monk's doorway at the south-east corner from a cloister, and is at first lost in gloom.   At last the great black columns, with their elaborate gilt ornamentation (the one decoration they understand in Siam), grow out in the feeble light from the little narrow windows in the low side walls.   The lofty peaked roof, which rises far into blackness, comes down gradually, sloping less steeply to the columns, of which there are two rows, and so to the low walls, thus as it were

covering a nave and side aisles. At the eastern end are placed the
usual gilt statues of Buddha, of all shapes and sizes—of which in one
cloister alone I saw over thirty-six over 3 feet high. Until these force
themselves upon one's notice with all the tawdry wreckage with

WAT CHINARETH (CENTRAL TOWER FROM WEST).

which they are ornamented, the air of retirement about the place is
quite captivating. The central tower is some 60 feet high, covered
with niches, in which stand more "prahs," or statues, and on the
eastern side is a staircase up halfway to a dome-shaped chamber.

The entrance to this was in its day very prettily panelled and gilded;
now, alas! cobwebs and bats are legion.   But the whole effect, there
almost lost in jungle, is memorable.

At a smaller wat to the southward (wat Boria) there is a very
fine Buddha, on whose head and shoulders the light is thrown from

A SALA IN THE NAN FORESTS.

a small window in the roof.   The effect is quite impressive, and
does great credit to the architect who designed it.   This is by no
means the only place in Siam where the light is dexterously managed.

Throughout this country the rivers, streams, and canals (or klongs)

KORAT PLATEAU.   ENTRANCE TO FOREST DONG PHYA YEN.

are the highways, and the villages are built on their edge; the banks,
owing to the accumulations, the houses, and the preservative effect of
the palms in which the villages nestle, are often the highest points in
the country round—which in the rains becomes a series of vast lakes,
with islands here and there, and the houses standing out of the water
gaunt upon their long stilt-like piles of teak.   In many parts the
buffaloes and oxen have to be driven away for miles to higher

ground; and one may meet whole villages moving with as many as forty ox-carts in a gang, with spare oxen trotting behind their masters' carts.

We had met a good deal of teak being rafted down the lower part of the river. The small rafts come through the innumerable klongs and creeks from all directions, and then below Pichit and Paknam Pho the big rafts are made up, and go off downwards with their crew of men, the cock crowing merrily on the roof of the little bamboo shelter which is their "deck-house." Passing sandbanks and shallows is often a very difficult operation. Some three or four men go overboard astern with long 8-feet stakes, to which the end of a long hawser is fast. The sharpened ends they drive into the bottom, clinging on to the top end as the strain comes on, till at last often it is too great, and the stake is pulled over man and all. However, by degrees they will bring the great floating mass to a standstill for the night, or, as the case may be, they succeed in checking the after end sufficiently

GORGE NAM PGOI.

to keep it to the current, while three or four more hands are working the long transverse-set oars at the fore end in the direction required, and two or three more will be using long poles to keep off the shallows; all hands shout lustily the whole time. By this process, repeated hour by hour, they travel slowly to Bangkok with the current.

Above Pichit we met but few rafts, and those only consisting of bamboo and "mai kabao," which is much used for small work, such as tables, and is brought down in small pieces, generally about 14 feet long.

Muang Pechai is the chief town of a very extensive and important province, which to the north-east reaches to the Mekong at Chieng Kan. The Governor, Phya Pechai, is a fine, tall young man, who is (and this is not too often the case in Siam) extremely popular with the people. His evident honesty of purpose was apparent the first moment he spoke. We had to stay here a few days to get the elephants together and buy rice. Twelve *kanan* (a coconut-shell) were selling at a *tical*, and on the average each man consumes one *kanan* per day. We laid in a stock of 35 *thang* (of 20 *kanan*), and were shortly after glad to get off on our journey towards the distant hills. I should add that this place is the starting-point for Paklai, on the Mekong, the trail between these two places being the route generally followed by the officials going to Luang Prabang. Apart from this it is not of much importance, and, situated in the uninteresting plain, is subject to high floods in the rains, as the water-marks on the piles of the post-office and the school and court houses attest.

Two days, passing through scrub jungle, brings the traveller to Ban Nam Pi, where there are some iron "mines"—a series of shallow diggings on an extensive deposit of limonite, which seems to be "derivative" from surface decomposition. The quartz rock, which generally underlies it, is probably a quartz sand which has been metamorphosed under pressure into the hard material we now find. In, or in close connection with the latter, the iron nodules are not to be found, but near the surface, where the quartz has softened and looks almost like a sandstone, the nodules occur in abundance.

The great difficulty was to get any one to do any work, even in clearing away *débris*, such is the fear of the " Pi," or spirits, who are said to guard the mineral. Without the offer of a white bullock, who ought first to be slain for their benefit, it was asserted that the spirits would certainly interfere with any one attempting to do any work. I was also told that when the iron ore is removed it brings bad luck to any house in which it is stored, and that, if hung up on a tree (certainly an odd place for stowing ores), it invariably causes the death of the tree. An iron-shod bamboo is the only tool used, but no work has been done for ages, and the small furnace which once existed at the village is quite dilapidated. It was quite vain setting to work myself, and giving out that I had made a permanent arrangement with all the " Pi," even the most vicious, before leaving Bangkok; nothing less than a royal proclamation will ever give the people confidence enough to make the opening up of these places possible.

On January 10 we were fairly under way for the north, high in hope and spirits, as a party always is when the scenery begins to change, and weary plains give way to lofty hill-ranges and distant peaks, with cool clear streams splashing in the rocky watercourses. At Muang Fang we came down to the Meinam once more, and camped in a very fine wat, which none of us will ever forget; for we marched in, parched and dusty, to find ourselves under orange trees loaded with fruit, and then and there all hands almost bathed in the delicious cool juice. To the south is a lovely semicircle of hills of schist, which turn the river away to the west. To the north, the timber-clad heights rose shoulder upon shoulder, far into the peaks of Kao Luet and Kao Taw, dim with distance. We were at last fairly in the mountains and in the Laos country.

I do not wish to give what would perhaps be a wearying account of our marches day after day, full of pleasure, of changing beauties, and of memorable incidents as they were, but as succinctly as possible to speak of the configuration of the country we passed through.

We next day forded the river at Ban Taluat, and were in the province of Nan. The trail on to Cherim (north-east) crosses a number of small hills of clay slate, which form the outlying buttresses of the rougher country to the north; the strike which I observed here and all the way up on our northerly journey is pretty regularly north and south, the dip westerly at about 25°, sometimes steeper. Water is scarce here, and when we stopped for breakfast in the bed of a *hoay* (or mountain-stream) at 9, after about three hours' going, even the holes in the sandy bed only gave us two or three pints of water; but, of course, in January this is to be expected. To avoid the rough country northward the trail crosses the Meinam once more, where its direction is southerly, to Cherim, whence the march to M. Faek is a very long and hilly one, over high ridges of clay slate, which carry one up over 1000 feet above the river. Some of the glimpses we got in the early mornings, as we climbed upwards among the tall trunks, were quite magnificent. These forests, in their winter clothing of reds and yellows, with the tall grey trunks standing out clear against the deep shadows behind, are, with the early morning or evening sun upon them, perfectly gorgeous. As day dawns the rays climb down the heights above you into the mists, which forthwith whirl and melt; and then, as you rise above it all, there lies below on all sides a billowy sea of wild forest, high on jagged ridges in the sunlight, or darkened in shadows far down in the deep torrent valleys; in the

blue distance eastward the Nam Pat range lies dim, and north and
west the eye loses itself among endless cloud-capped ranges.

The sala at Muang Faek is on the west side of the river, and
consists of a number of separate bamboo shelters; here we had
to rest our elephants, all eighteen of which were tired out by the
climb from Cherim, and we had to engage two more to reduce the
weights on our tired beasts.   Elephants in Siam are never idle, and
the animals I got from Pechai, which belonged to the Minister of the
Mining Department, had all been hard at work hauling teak and such
things before our arrival.   At Muang Faek there are a good many,
and the two which now joined us were a male and female of
magnificent proportions.   They had a swinging gait, with which they
travelled much faster than the others, evidently not being accustomed
to dragging heavy timber, but to light weights and hard climbing.
At first they didn't like their new surroundings at all, and it was
most curious to see how, when the one began to trumpet and back
out of the crowd, the other rushed up, caressing him with her trunk
all over, and even pushing it into his mouth, and stood by him till
he was pacified; but if she left his side for a moment, round he
whirled in search of her, and the mahout could do nothing to stop
him.   I never saw them separated by more than twenty yards the
whole time they were with us; they had always to be loaded and
unloaded together, as they stood side by side, entwining their trunks
lovingly, and in the evening, after the march, they bathed together
and squirted one another in huge enjoyment.   The howdahs are
simply rough saddles like big baskets, and are generally fitted with
a close plaited roof with a long peak before and behind, like those
fitted on the *kiens,* or ox-carts, of the plains.

From M. Faek the trail, which is well trodden, passes along
the steep wooded banks of the Meinam, which, however, is here
known as the Nam Nan.   The clay slate dips 65° W., and makes
long black ridges in the river-bed, which can be seen deep down in
the clear water, or rising in sharp crags above it, and forming the
rapids, which make the river a difficult highway at the best, and only
navigable by the long narrow dug-outs.

It is a short march to Hoay Li, where there is a sala kept, as
they all are in Nan, in excellent condition; but there is a stream
close by.   The next day's march was a heavy one, over more lofty ridges
without water, and it is, therefore, a good stopping-place.   Leaving

at sunrise, the Laos guide and myself reached the small shelter at Hoay Nai at one o'clock, the rest of my Siamese straggling in well blown an hour later, and the elephants climbing down the steep water-course at three. This is generally the extent of a day's march, and the average rate of jungle-travelling, allowing for stoppages, is never over 2½ miles an hour, and a six hours' march is as much as the Siamese can do; in these hills the elephants certainly do not do more than 2 miles an hour. To the Laos trotting along on foot there is, however, no limit that I ever discovered, even with the heavy loads which they carry swung on a pole across the shoulder. With a couple of handfuls of *kao nëo*, the hill-rice, which they steam over a pot into a glutinous mass, very handy and portable for the day's march, and with some dried fish and a banana, and a long pull at the fresh stream water once in the day, they will go cheerily from morn till night, swinging when necessary their long *dhâp* (a sword of Burmese style, which every man over sixteen carries if he be a man at all), to cut and lop the branches and jungle which are for ever blocking the tracks. This stopping-place was one of the wildest we were ever in; nothing but jungle and mountains all around, the place itself a tiny clearing in the bottom of a deep narrow ravine, where the monster trunks climbed far above us, leaving only one little space of open sky, from which at three o'clock the sun was shut out, and where at half-past five night had fairly set in. A number of gangs going south from Nan were camped here with us.

Another, easy, march brought us to Muang Hin, over 1200 feet above sea-level. Imagine a number of lovely villages clustering among their coconut and areca palms, in a beautiful wide valley surrounded by forests and hills, the glistening yellow paddy-stalks bright in the afternoon sun, with the black backs of the buffalo moving lazily about; the homely red of the little oxen, and the moving islands the elephants make whisking the paddy in their trunks; with the village sounds drifting down the quiet air—the distant drum at the monastery, whose grey roof stands above the other houses, or the far-off "poot, poot" of the "nok poot" in the jungle (a black bird, by the way, with a long pheasant-like tail and light red wings)—and you have an idea of the lovely scene which spread before us that evening as we emerged from the hills.

This valley runs parallel to the Nam Nan valley to the east-ward, but drains in exactly the opposite direction, the water running

C

north and turning into the Nam Nan considerably north of M. Sisaket.
Three days going down this lovely valley brought us through a
rough piece of limestone country to Muang Sa, where I stayed
some days visiting several places in the neighbourhood. This township is important, and stands by the Nam Nan in a very fine paddy-
growing plain, and is better supplied with inhabitants than the

THE PADDY-FIELDS, HIN VALLEY.

country we had come through; but even here the tigers are very bold,
and often come right into the villages. Small irrigation canals extend
in all directions.

Like the quarrymen in North Wales, whenever there is a cry of
" gold " at Clogan, the Laos take every piece of yellow copper pyrites
or iron pyrites for gold, and we had several very hard days' travelling
both east and west after gold-mines of this description.

The minimum readings for the last five days were 62°, 49°, 46°,
43°, and 45° Fahr., and going on one day's march over the plain to
Muang Nan, the capital of this great province, we had 60° as minimum
for several days.

The salas stand outside the red-brick walls of Nan, and are only
a few hundred yards from the river, and here was every sign of
prosperity; every other family seems to own an elephant or two.
The houses are well built and enclosed in stout palisades; and besides
the town inside the walls, there is a very large number of houses
between them and the river. I saw numbers of dug-outs arriving
with cotton, and many too going away south. There are a few Burmese
shopkeepers along the east wall, their principal stock consisting of
check-patterned *panungs* and *sarongs* and small knickknacks, betel
boxes, and a little silver-work. A mule caravan of Haws from the

north—as dirty and ugly as the dirtiest Chinamen—were also anxious to sell Chinese slippers, sheepskin coats, walnuts and sandals, and shortly after left for the south, like others we had met at Muang Sa. From M. Sa I gathered they were going to make westward toward

WAT BEN YEUN, M. SA.

M. Pray. Some of the Burmese brought me some sapphires from Chieng Kong, and there were some fine stones, but I was at the time surprised to find they had no rubies. Coloured quartzes are also found in this neighbourhood, and are cut for ornament. The

EAST GATE OF NAN.

rupee is the current coin, and the Burmese shopkeepers and a China-man or two were the only people who would exchange our money for us—at the rate of three salung to the rupee.

The sight of Nan is the early morning market, to which before sunrise the women are seen coming from all directions, wrapped in their long plaids—for such, indeed, the Lao cloak is, both in pattern and mode of wearing. The market is held within the walls in the open

c 2

space, in which stands the *sanam*, or court-house ; this is surrounded on three sides by wats, and on the west by the palace, a large house with no very striking features.   The women crouch along the sides in rows with their baskets in front of them, as at Luang Prabang and at all the markets one sees in this part of the peninsula.   Fruit, biscuits, and cakes, ready rolled cigarettes and flowers, are for sale, but the quantities are very small.   There is a muffled sound of subdued chatter and laughter, and the scene is a very pretty one—till at last the mists are gone, the sun is well up in the heavens, and the crowd melts away as silently as it came.

Once inside the walls the town may be described as countrified, the houses standing in their own enclosures among their palms, where the

 elephants twirl their trunks among the cocks and hens.   Very fair roads run at right angles to one another, but are always quiet and shady, like country lanes.   The chief business seems

LAOS BAG, OF STRIPED CLOTH.   KAO NEO WICKER BASKETS.

to be outside the town, villages extending on all sides, and especially along the road to the north, past the "old city," which is about one mile in that direction, and where there are some very good substantial palisades still standing, with the remains of a deep ditch and massive wall on the north-west side, all of course very much grown over.   The custom of shaving the head all round, with the exception of the tuft at the top which stands bristling straight on end, and gives a good grip to the light-red or white turban which is often worn, is a cool and cleanly one, and gives the men a smart appearance; the black tattooing, which extends from the knee up to the middle of the body, is the other distinctive feature throughout the province of Nan. They seldom wear more than the panung and a short blue jacket, except in the early mornings, when, with the thermometer at 50°, they shiver inside their long plaids; as the day becomes warmer, the plaid is rolled up and stowed in the bag, which is as indispensable as the *dhâp*, and goes over one shoulder, carrying its owner's all—consisting of a small basket of *kao neo* for the day, some tobacco, and betel-nut, with often a long-stemmed pipe and flint and steel.

The women tie their long hair up on the top of their heads, and when I first got among them I was reminded of the same fashion at home, as also by other points of resemblance one had not seen among the Siamese—a light springy step, a pleasant-sounding voice, a well-cut figure, and a rosy cheek. In some of the districts in the hills the women suffer severely from goitre, and up the Nam Wa, a wild torrent which joins the Nam Nan from the east, just below

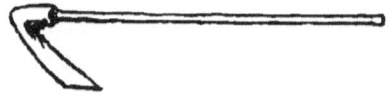

AXE FOR HOLLOWING BOATS.

DIPPER FOR WATER.

Muang Sa, three out of every four of the women I saw had it. Up that river, too, I noticed a lack of expression in the faces of the men and lads when in repose; but they are rare hands at a joke, and then their faces light up wonderfully. These men all wore short jackets to the waist, of blue cloth, leaving a strip of tattooing between it and the blue panung. I was astonished at the number of children I saw there, too, every man we met in the jungle having some four or five of his sons with him. Ten or even fifteen children is a number not uncommon for one woman, while in Siam, as a rule, the number three is not exceeded. I imagine the population must be now recovering from the effects of the continual warfare which existed before Siam made its rule felt in the north, and which no doubt accounts for the meagre population throughout the entire peninsula.

Of the joyful, kindly, and hospitable character of the Laos of Nan one cannot say too much; I never saw a surly face or heard an angry word. Their honesty is proverbial, and they are singularly temperate: drinking *lao* (which is distilled from rice to a large extent in Siam itself), smoking opium, theft, and malice seem to have no attractions for them. I believe every one who has travelled with and among them will say the same, and will ever keep their memory stowed away in a warm corner of the heart.

The Rachawong was the official I saw most of—an upstanding, refined, and gentlemanly looking man, with a touch of iron grey in his hair, a firm step, a strong mouth, and high clear forehead. He gave me the story of some recent trouble with Chow Sa (the Prince of Sa) without any of that repetition, detail, or tinge of animosity one expects from an uneducated or inferior mind when speaking of an enemy.

Preparations were beginning for the cremation of the late "king" who was just dead, but we left before the ceremony began.

The punishment of death, which was inflicted for opium-smoking, elephant-killing, or theft, has been replaced during the last few years by a milder form; but it is noteworthy that in two years only one man has been put in the prison at Nan.

The music is a great contrast to that of the Siamese. At a dinner to which I was invited at M. Sa, we had, to an accompaniment of three bamboo flutes with very sweet low tones, a kind of duet sung by two girls, each taking a verse in turn. The rather nasal notes would soar up quite independently of the flutes, and then suddenly return to the keynote, which was a lovely minor, and was sustained; then would come a pause, with the delightful subdued refrain on the flutes again, ere the other began. The subject was a war-song, on which they both extemporized; but even my Siamese could not follow the words at all. After a solo from one of the flutists, who, as usual, sang falsetto (which is especially affected by the Siamese too in love-songs), he and one of the damsels lighted tapers, and though in no dress but their ordinary open dark blue jackets of panung, they performed another kind of duet, accompanied by waving of hands and arms, and a certain amount of not ungraceful attitudinizing. It seemed to be a kind of sacred affair, with a slow dignified air, and they quite lost themselves in it, though some of my Siamese were making running comments in the usual style of the vulgar all over the world.

As far as music goes, it was far more expressive and peaceful than anything I had heard in Siam, as the others owned. I had with me as assistant-surveyor a very accomplished young Siamese, who is an excellent specimen of the best that Siam produces; he is a capital musician after the fashion of his country, and used continually to warble languishing love-airs to our great amusement, and also good marching airs. He had a good ear, and soon picked up some of the Laos tunes, and so one had good opportunities of comparing them. It was curious, too, how he and several of the others took to English airs they heard from me, even copying the sounds of the English words. The proficiency of the Siamese "service" bands in Bangkok shows, too, that they can master and appreciate our music.

I have heard the Laos called "savages," which can only be said in ignorance. They respect superiors, are devoted to their "chows," to whom they are united by feudal ties, are obedient to their parents, extremely hospitable, and perfectly honest. The stranger to them is no enemy, but a creature that needs kindness, and invariably gets it. Quarrelling is unknown. They respect their women, and, unlike the Siamese, walk behind them and bear the heaviest load. They do the jungle-work, and the women stay at home, weaving their silk panungs or their horizontally striped petticoats at the loom beneath the house; while the dogs, no longer vile pariahs, but cared for well, and of a breed something like a sheepdog, sit by and watch the children play.

Surely there is something besides savagery here.

PART II.

MUANG NAN TO MUANG CHIENG KONG.

FROM Muang Nan my orders were to find the best route I could over the watershed to M. Chieng Kong in the Mekong valley. As usual, the information obtainable was very meagre. One trail goes west from Nan till the valley of the Nam Ing is reached, when that stream is followed down north; a second follows the Nam Nan northward, and crosses the range north-north-westerly up the stream flowing down from M. Yao; the third, which I selected, as showing one more of the Nam Nan valley, follows that river up as far north as M. Ngob (lat. 19° 29′), when the direction becomes north-westerly over the rough country which brings one to M. Chieng Hon and M. Chieng Kob.

Leaving Nan on February 1, we followed a good tract among low but precipitous and picturesque limestone hills, into a curiously disforested country, where the only growth was bamboo, until we dropped suddenly upon the river once more at Pak Ngao, where we camped on the sandbank. We had by this time picked up, as one does in the East, a considerable following. A Commissioner had been sent across from Chieng Mai to accompany me up to Chieng Kong. What his actual duties were I never discovered; he was very useful, however, in helping me in various ways, but I would willingly have done without him, for he was evidently one of that class of officials who grind the people very tight when their superiors are out of sight. Another, the brother of Chow Sa, by name Chow Benn Yenn, who was with me all the time from Muang Sa until I reached Bangkok again, was the greatest contrast to the former. He was a small, neatly made fellow of about twenty-one, a splendid forest man, who, though a great swell in these parts, travelled with only three or four lads with him, and could walk the whole expedition off their legs. He knew and could imitate exactly every forest

sound, and as he trotted along the trail he gathered all kinds of
unlikely looking plants, which in the evening made excellent
additions to our curry. He was a born sportsman, and far
more at his ease sleeping out at night under his plaid, with his lads
stretched round him, than under any form of roof. The lads with
him—for they were mere boys—were like him, and treated him with
the usual freedom and familiarity peculiar to the Laos, but which
if an order was given, disappeared before complete obedience;
and if the Chow wanted a drink of water or half a handful of *kao-
neo*, they would go miles or give their last crumbs to supply him,
and many were the generous and willing kindnesses I had to thank
them for.

We had also an official with his sons and a few men to carry
their loads from Nan, who acted as guides and a kind of walking
letter of introduction everywhere. They were a remarkably handsome
lot, but the old fellow himself used to come in very done up after
the day's march. Yet, like all the rest, he was never put out by
hunger or weariness, and would take his bag off his shoulder, throw
down his long dhâp, and squat on his heels and laugh again to think
that he should be tired and the youngsters not.

From Pak Ngao, where we saw a few dug-outs shooting past down
the rapids, we next day passed over more of this disforested limestone country, the dip of the rocks being westerly and very steep
(50° to 60°), until we forded the river below M. Saipum. We passed
through a number of villages, with very pretty whitewashed
monasteries, and high palisades round them; the view to the north-
east was a novel one, for the usual foreground of yellow fields, with
its dykes and ditches, and its many watch-houses reared high on
piles, was backed not by forest, but by open expanses, with trees
here and there, or low bamboo scrub, and a dwarf range of bare
hills behind. There is a red sandstone which seems to underlie the
limestone, and wherever that rock outcrops, the soil is excessively
thin and poor, and the denuding power of the rains is very marked.
That often accounts for low scrub jungle; but where that is not
present, as in the limestone country we had just crossed, the absence
of forest must, I fancy, be due to fires; and no doubt when a fire
is lit for the purpose of clearing ground for the hill rice, it will,
with a good breeze, clear square miles instead of acres. I saw a
great deal of this burning going on subsequently in the Mekong

valley, and I never saw results commensurate with the destruction caused.

The sala at M. Lim, where we slept, is on the east bank, the town being opposite, and the " Chow Muang " or Governor came wading over with the water up to his neck, and his clothes in a bundle on his head. There are numbers of very fine ducks here, but, as usual, we had great difficulty in getting any in exchange for money. They have not great use for money here, as they themselves say, and they prefer their ducks. This happens constantly, especially when buying rice. Each village has enough for its consumption for the year, and very often no more; and naturally they prefer to keep the necessaries of life to having comparatively useless silver buried under their house. As the country is opened up, this will no doubt change, but at present it is not worth their while to grow more than they can consume themselves.

Again, a few irresponsible travellers have been in the habit of provisioning themselves at the expense of the villages without paying, and the consequence is that when a European appears (or, indeed, often a Siamese official), there is a general stampede into the jungle, and everything is hidden away, for they expect nothing but robbery at his hands. Until, after infinite pains, they are persuaded that they will be dealt honestly by, and treated with the consideration which the wildest from their own hills would never fail to show, you can get nothing but negatives, and small blame to them. It is humiliating in the extreme, after travelling with men for some weeks, to be asked one night over the camp fire why the *nai farang* (the foreign master) doesn't kick and thrash the men on the march, or flog the Chow Muang into handing over all the rice in the village, and do other not less objectionable things. Yet such is the conduct expected of one, as a matter of course, from the past repute of the *farang* which travels far, and no doubt also does suffer from exaggeration. Still, it shows what our methods too often have been. With these people you get the measure you mete to them; firmness is first of all necessary, but brutality is lowering to all concerned, and never has done anything but harm, and is more far-reaching than the contemptible authors of it understand.

Another day's march through a good deal of evergreen brings one, after crossing the Nam Pur, flowing in from the east, to M. Chieng Kan. An hour further north is M. Chieng Klan; and the confusion of the two names is endless. The latter is the better stopping-place, though the former is very prettily situated, on the bank of the Nam Nan, among very fine clumps of bamboo and a great many banana palms and sugar-cane plantations. Of the latter every man slings a couple of stalks over his shoulder for the day's journey, and most refreshing they are. The cakes of brown sugar made from them, of which one generally takes a piece or two to give a taste to the *kao neo,* are not considered good for the digestion, and quite rightly, and so only. just enough is taken at a time to give a taste. The sugar from the sugar palm of the plains, however, never has any evil results, and

A HILL MONASTERY, M. LE.

as it has a pleasant flavour, when we got back to it in the Khorat plateau, we consumed large quantities.

The next day M. Le was reached over sandy, undulating jungle country. On foot one could easily have reached M. Ngob, but the elephants could not do it, being, as I mentioned before, in bad condition. I was not loth to rest the night here, it being one of the most beautiful of the hill-enclosed valleys we had been in. From the sala we looked out over the terraced paddy fields, with the winding silver of the river below, and abruptly beyond it shoulder upon shoulder of heavily timbered ranges rising into the peaks which divided us from the Chieng Hon plain to the west and north-west. Eastward, and just over us, were low steep hills, on a spur of which was a small hill monastery, whence the bells on the gables sent down a gentle tinkling as they were swayed by the strong south-westerly breeze which was sweeping a watery rustling sound out of the bamboos and coconut palms.

The salas being small, the people of the village ran up in half an hour one of their bamboo lean-to shelters for the men, but the Laos as usual seemed to prefer lighting a fire and lying out in the open round it in their cloaks, there being always one man sitting up on watch and supplying fuel when necessary.

M. Ngob is in a narrow hollow, which I should not care to visit in hot weather, for the wind hardly gets into the place. We had nearly a whole day's rest here. A mule caravan of Haws came in from the north and rendered the otherwise peaceful air hideous with their loud, hoarse talking. But for them a Laos village is singularly quiet; no sounds but the quack, quack of the fat ducks who share the pools in the stream with a few laughing children, the grunts of a family of pigs, the occasional trumpet of an elephant who has been up to some playful game or other of which the master does not approve, and the steady thump, thump of the small foot rice mills, which the women work apparently from morn till night.

Before sunrise, as the sonorous chant rises from the wat, these mills are at work too, and often the last thing at night one hears them still. Mr. McCarthy has described them, but I may just mention that they consist of a piece of tree-trunk hollowed into a funnel-shape, into which the rice is put, and a long lever worked at the outer end by the foot, the woman stepping on and off, fitted with a hammer-head of wood, of which several of different sizes are used. And while the mother works her loom close by, the two daughters will work the mill and chat and chaff the passers-by.

Minimum readings for the last four days, 52°, 55°, 57°, 58° Fahr. The maximum in one of these salas is generally about 82° for this month at 2 to 3 p.m. The winds were now south-westerly, very strong, with bright fierce sun, but cumuli lying on the higher peaks after 4 p.m., sometimes a slight shower falling from them.

One mile north-west from M. Ngob, the Nam Nan,* here known as the Nam Ngob (and actually the people did not know that it was the same river as the Nam Nan below), runs over shallow pebble beds, where we forded to the west side. This day's march is a very good example of the kind of travelling to be done. The tracks over

---

* The river evidently takes its rise from Doi Luang (a large hill mass south of M. Hongsawadi), 19° 35′ N., 101° 24′ E.

the hills are either in the bed of the " hoays," or streams, far down in a perpetual night, where the coldness of the water chills the feet and legs through and through ; or, after a steep climb, high up on narrow spurs leading to the central range, where the forest is thick enough to keep off all the wind but not the rays of the sun after 10 a.m. Once on these ridges no water is to be had for half a day, and the stick of sugar-cane or water-bottle of cold tea, the best of all beverages, is worth its weight in gold.   However, drinking on the march is a

VIEW FROM M. LE, LOOKING NORTH-WEST ACROSS THE NAM NAN AND WATERSHED
OF MEINAM KHONG.

ruinous habit.   The Laos sensibly rinse the mouth when they can, and only drink at the end of the day.

Following up Hoay Sakeng over red sandstone rocks, the track then climbs on to a long ridge, leading, with many rises and falls, to a small gap in the range, about 1100 feet above the river.   We met on the way four pack oxen coming, with their pretty deep-toned bell, down the path, and on reaching the summit had a most glorious view of the thick forests of the Chieng Hon valley, with the small clearings here and there and surrounded on all sides, as far as one could see in the dim haze which accompanies the south-west wind, by hill ranges.   Twenty minutes down a steep drop at a run brought us into a different climate and the most perfect valley I was ever in. Far above, the sun glistened here and there on the wide-spreading fronds of huge tree-ferns; for the rest, we were almost in darkness, with orchids and great twisted creepers climbing on the tree-trunks dim above us. The stream is known as Hoay Tok, and down its bed we stumbled, cutting ourselves about on the rough outcrops, the strike of which, with a steep westerly dip, was at right angles to our course, and made most unpleasant travelling. Two hours more across a partially cultivated plain, and we passed another Haw caravan encamped, and reached the sala. The elephants did not arrive until 5 p.m., it having taken them twelve hours to reach M. Chieng Hon.

At M. Pechai I had bought some ponies. There are not many there, and the choice was limited, while the price, forty to sixty ticals, was heavy. These animals, as long as we were in flat country, were useful, but they were not good mountaineers, and I found travelling on foot much pleasanter, while, as a general rule, the more exercise men get in these jungles, the healthier they are. On this day each one of my Siamese assistants had a fall, for they, as a rule, stuck to their ponies' backs, whatever the trail was like; this often means getting one's face and hands tremendously knocked about, frequent dismountings, slow progress, and endless bother, while it also stands in the way of surveying or careful observation of the lie of the ground.

There was a very heavy, damp mist when we pushed on next day through the Dong Choi, a magnificent forest, which almost covers this plateau with the scenery of Hoay Tok continued, only on a larger and more imposing scale. The size of the ferns, and especially of the hart's-tongues, which clung in masses, with clumps of orchids, far up on the bare trunks of the trees which form the roofing of branch and leaf above, was quite astonishing to me.

Camp was made by a small sala in a wild clearing at Sala Pangue, from which the sun was early excluded by the hills and forest on the west, which we were to cross on the morrow. The tired elephants had a well-earned afternoon's rest. To give them time to get in before sunset, next day we got under way at 3.30 a.m., every six or eight men having a torch about eight feet long of split bamboo. These early marches are a sort of scrambling dream, and should not be resorted to except under compulsion, as, although the cool morning air is pleasant for the first hour, every one soon gets very done up, and stumbles on hazily. Sunrise puts new life into one, but the want of the early morning sleep makes one feel the heat of the day far more. Moreover, of course, nothing of the country is seen.

We rose for an hour and a half up over hills, and one or two of the ponies had some tremendous falls, and were soon left struggling behind. At sunrise we were descending once more among the wildest and most rugged scenes into the valley of Nam Pote, and were now fairly in the Mekong drainage. This was another of the wonderful valleys which are so common here; and the temperature was just over 10° Fahr. below that of the hill ridges when we left them at 6 a.m. About 8.30, after crossing and recrossing the stream about thirty times, and being regularly chilled, I stopped at a small sala, and was glad to bask in the sun. An hour and a half later the others came up, and we breakfasted. Chow Benn Yenn's sharp eyes had seen some deer and two tigers, but they were off in a moment. Where the former is the latter follows, but neither will stay when he detects the sound of man coming through the forest. The tiger takes the greatest trouble to avoid a man, unless very famished. Often then he is rendered bold enough to attack a solitary man, when squatting down to eat his *kao neo*, and it is thus that accidents occur; but he will seldom face two men, and that is why one always meets the Laos in couples, if not in greater numbers.

At 10.30 we continued down the valley; rock apparently red sandstone, but so decomposed at its outcrop as to give no clue of reliable character. Passed numbers of wild banana trees, which do not bear fruit. They are very aggravating to tired men, who hear the cry of a jungle fowl, and coming round a corner see the broad leaves of the bananas; naturally we jump forward, thinking to get a rest and a bunch of bananas, and, perhaps, a fowl or some eggs for the evening's supper, but find nothing and no sign of man or fowl.

The course is roughly north-west until the hills fall back, and the valley opens on a flat piece of paddy land, bounded north and south by lofty limestone rocks, with, to the west, a barrier caused by a steep north and south ridge, over which lies M. Kob, but round which a long *detour* has to be made to the north-west, down the Nam Pote valley, to where the Nam Kob meets it. Passing Ban Tam, Ban Prow, and Ban Faek, prosperous-looking villages, we reached the junction at one o'clock. After a brief rest in the shade, in another hour and a half, after fording Nam Kob pretty frequently (making about the ninetieth time we had been in the water that day), we reached the sala of M. Kob. The others began to arrive about four

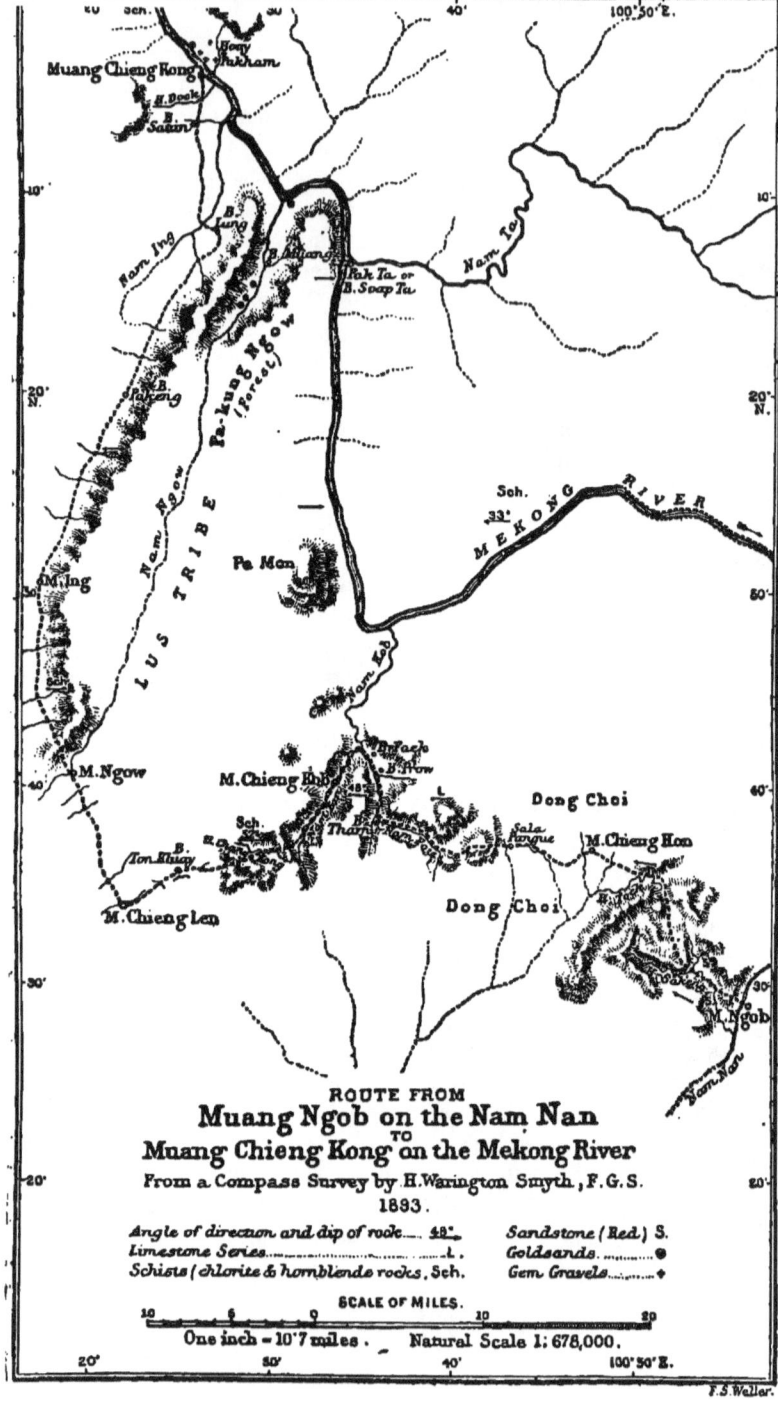

ROUTE FROM
Muang Ngob on the Nam Nan
TO
Muang Chieng Kong on the Mekong River

From a Compass Survey by H. Warington Smyth, F.G.S.
1893.

Angle of direction and dip of rock .... 48°.   Sandstone (Red) S.
Limestone Series .... L.   Goldsands .... ●
Schists (chlorite & hornblende rocks, Sch.   Gem Gravels .... +

SCALE OF MILES.

One inch = 10·7 miles .   Natural Scale 1: 678,000.

F.S.Weller.

o'clock, and the elephants at 6.30, looking very sorry ; and we had to give them a complete rest next day.

From the character of the scenery here, and at the top of the Nam Pote, where we struck it, I imagine the hills we came down among were limestones overlying the sandstone again ; all round the Muang are the wildest and most fantastic peaks, and, with the steep heights hanging immediately over it, it was more like a Norwegian valley than anything I have seen.

The wats here are very simple, the houses neat, but small ; bricks are baked in the valley, and the rice-mills thump cheerily and echo off the hills all day. There were some pack oxen, which came over from the westward ; but the Laos who drove them, whether from distrust of us or not, I do not know, would not converse with any of us. The bells of these caravans as they go trotting down the valleys are beautiful. First goes a large, deep-toned bell, swinging between the packs of the leader ; the next is a third above it ; and the rear is brought up by a treble bell. The little oxen trot in their order without other guidance than that of the bells and an occasional shout, one man leading, another to every five animals, and one to bring up the rear. The baskets are hung on each side of the hump, with often an ornamental erection between them ; there are fore and aft stays of leather, and these prevent the packs coming off when the animals are climbing. We had met some before—and met and used others afterwards ; however pretty they look as they trot along, their bells tinkling far over land and forest, they are not pleasant to travel with, especially in the rains, when streams are all in flood, for it is impossible to keep anything they carry at all dry.

While we were resting here a fire occurred, and two houses were burnt to the ground in about seven minutes. My Siamese, I must say, worked very well and pluckily, the Laos seeming quite dazed by the catastrophe. We cut down a row of banana palms, split up the trunks, and threw them on the flames, by the water and moisture in them beating down the fire, so that two neighbouring houses were saved, with the outhouses, in which, in huge bins, the rice was stored. For this last the poor fellows who only arrived home at night to find their houses burned, were most grateful ; they came to thank us, and I was very much struck with the conduct of my people, who, beginning with my boat-boy, a Mon, or Peguan (who at the fire and on every other occasion had shown himself a very smart, handy, and good-

D

hearted fellow), selected what clothes they could spare, and sent the two Laos men away loaded with raiment, and with tears of thankfulness in their eyes. It gives an additional pleasure to work with men who can act like that.

Thermometer readings on the march from Sala Pangue were— 3 a.m., 42° Fahr.; 5.30 a.m., on the hills, 60°; 6·30 a.m., in Nam Pote valley, 50°; 9 a.m., ditto, 59°; noon, in the shade, Ban Faek, 87° Fahr. My aneroids had both been injured by my careless people, and I could get no reliable heights.

From M. Kob the trail follows up the Nam Tan in a general south-south-west direction, and crosses a low watershed into the bed of the Hoay Chang Kong, another rocky stream disastrous to foot gear. It then crosses low ridges and jungle, passing several small villages to Ban Ton Kluay, 6½ hours' walk, though most of the people took 8, and the elephants over 9.

Thermometer minimum—54° at sunrise in heavy damp mist; strong south-westerly breeze at noon; thick haze all day.

Six hours from here, over flat country, past M. Chieng Len, and in a general north-north-west direction from that place is M. Ngau, which gives its name to the Nam Ngau flowing north-north-east to the Mekong, and meeting it half a day's boat journey below Chieng Kong. We met a number of traders from the north carrying their loads; they were smoking long-stemmed pipes, and looked very Burmese in face. They wore blue sailor-looking trousers, with red trimmings round the ankle, where they were very loose, and small blue jackets with bead trimmings, while some had marvellously wide straw hats; with their uniformity of dress and its high colouring they made a very pretty picture crossing the yellow paddy fields.

The Chet Muang at Chieng Len was in trouble with the Nan authorities because he is, unfortunately, under the disaffected Chow Sa, and far away from there as he is, and utterly ignorant, as he protested, of his proceedings, it seemed likely that he would be involved in the disgrace of his chief.

From M. Ngau the trail crosses the upper end of the long range which forms the watershed of the Nam Ing and Nam Ngau, along the western side of which for three days we travelled, sleeping at Muang Ing and Ban Pakeng. From the latter place, leaving at a quarter to two in the morning, Ban Lung was reached at a quarter to seven. Here we forded Nam Ing, and crossed a burning plain almost

entirely devoid of vegetation for four hours more, and then in a huge
and very comfortable sala disposed of the contents of our haversacks
with the pleasant feeling of having reached our goal. Chow Benn
Yenn meanwhile had left us for a day or two's visiting at some other
villages east of Nam Ing which owed allegiance to Chow Sa. Con-
sequently, when I got in, there were only the Laos guide, my Mon
boatman, and two lusty young Siamese servants who had kept up ;
and, absurd as it may seem to Western ideas, the Chieng Kong people
took some hours to believe that I was come on genuine Government
business; for a man is measured in these parts according to the
number of his following, and until the men and elephants turned
up I was often looked at askance. This was sometimes very amusing
and sometimes not, especially when trying to procure coconuts or
bananas ! The sense of hospitality was, however, generally quick to
prevail.

The three days from Muang Ngau were through forest, the
villages lying mostly on our west in the flat land nearer the river.
We passed several forest fires, which where they approached the trail
made very hot travelling.

The barrenness of the country between the Nam Ing at Ban
Lung and Chieng Kong seems to have been originally caused by
fires. The only cultivation was by a muddy stream at Ban Satan,
a name which struck me as particularly appropriate in such a
wilderness. There is an absence of water, I was afterwards told,
which prevents cultivation of any value, and owing to this the
Burmese gem-diggers have given up trying to follow indications of
stones on this side.

The first view of the Mekong fairly took one's breath away, the
water here spreading out into a wide placid river of half a mile in
width, winding slowly away among a few sandbanks until lost in
the hills to the south-east. Across, on the north, lies a long low
series of hills, from which the gem-bearing Hoays seem all to take
their rise.

Thermometer minimum last four days—59°, 64°, 60°, 58° ;
maximum in sala, 90°, very thick haze all day, with strong breezes
from south towards noon.

PART III.

MUANG CHIENG KONG TO MUANG LUANG PRABANG.

MUANG CHIENG KONG became our head-quarters for ten days, and from there I made a boat expedition to the Chieng Sen boundary, north-west; and also one north and east inland, the object being the examination of the gem deposit, its extent, character, and, if possible, its value.

From the Chieng Sen boundary at Hoay Nam Kung, extending for some miles towards Chieng Kong, is a rapid piece of river tearing through a series of gneissose and schistose rocks, which form high hills on either bank. The gem-bearing gravel is not found until several basalt sheets are encountered below Nam Ngau, a largish tributary flowing in from the north. The hills on the left bank then become lower and more distant, and these, consisting of a dark crystalline rock, the exact mineralogical character of which has not yet been determined, seem to be the source of all the stone-bearing gravels which are found deposited in the streams flowing from them. The average thickness of the gravel is 5 to 20 inches, and consists of quartz and fragments of the crystalline rock above mentioned. The overburden is a reddish clay soil of an average depth of 10 feet, through which the Burmese, who are found wherever there are gems, sink large pits some 10 feet square. A sharpened bamboo will be often first driven down to ascertain if the gravel underlies the spot, it having been found very capricious.

Explorations were made in the neighbourhood for many years before—about two years ago—the first paying gravel was found; the Burmese relying all the time on the presence of what is known as *nin*, small black stones which have turned out to be black spinel, and are always to be found in close proximity to the sapphire. When washing gravel in a stream these little water-worn crystals are found; it will only need industry and time to find the gem gravel, which will be somewhere near, although in part perhaps denuded away. The *nin* have been followed for years, and now there are over two hundred men reaping the reward of their indefatigable patience. I found *nin* and struck gravel in all the streams flowing in on the left bank between Nam Ngau and Hoay Pakham, which is the main scene of the operations at present, and lies about 1 mile below Chieng Kong. On the right bank there are apparently no signs whatever, except at Hoay Duk, a stream exactly opposite Hoay Pakham; but only a few *nin* are to be seen here, and there is no water for washing purposes. East and north of Hoay Pakham, again, are half a dozen more streams flowing, from that side of the range I have spoken of as the source of the gravel, into the Nam Hau,

A GEM-DIGGER'S CLEARING, CHIENG KONG.

which eventually reaches the Mekong. Some of these have been found to be rich, and on one the Burmese built their bamboo villages and made their clearings; but after a fortnight's work the places were abandoned as being terribly unhealthy, sunk deep in the jungle valleys, and very difficult to get stores to.

When the present large workings are exhausted, both those and the streams towards Nam Ngau will get their fair share of attention, no doubt. The distance between the extreme points where the gravel exists and the limit of our present knowledge is over 10 miles, but within that area it is not by any means continuous, and any attempt at estimating the probable output and the extent of reserves could only result in the most erroneous conclusions. Owing to the secrecy observed by the Burmese in the matter among themselves, and the fact that they usually travel long distances to find a market for their better stones, the output up to the present of saleable stones is merely a matter of conjecture, and is variously estimated by the headmen as from 3 to 6 catties, say, over 22,000 carats perhaps. One man showed me what he declared was the result of his year's work—three good stones of rich colour and good water, for which he expected to get 100, 60, and 50 Rs. respectively, and some forty small ones (some of them of very poor colour), which after an hour's bargaining one could certainly have got for 50 Rs. He had, besides, of course, numberless fragments and scraps which were valueless. The chances are, from what I saw, that this is a fair example of what the average digger obtains; but it must be remembered that no information voluntarily given by the Burmese on this head is ever reliable. They invariably keep something in reserve, for they never feel quite certain what the Englishman may be up to with his questioning; and even among themselves the dodges resorted to to hide the exact truth are very amusing. In buying stones one always has the worst produced first, and after an exhaustive pick out of them all, presently, slowly, out of infinite wraps of paper and cotton, come some better ones, and after an hour or so the best are produced, and probably this is the real extent of the man's stock; but if through impatience one closes the bargains too early, the best are never produced, but will be kept for the future, and will eventually be taken over to Rangoon, or even Calcutta.

In a few years' time there will, no doubt, be more men at work, and larger areas of pits in work. At the present moment the ground in Hoay Pakham has only been dug out for a distance of half a mile from the flood level of the Mekong, with a breadth averaging 80 yards. Work is only carried on in the morning, when the pit will be bailed out dry; at noon the digging and washing ceases, and the men return home, and sit all the afternoon in their houses chaffing, talking, and picking over and enjoying the sight of their stones, in which they find great delight. The washing consists simply of cleaning the basket of muddy gravel with water, and picking over the remains twice by hand. The operation is very quick, and the eye never misses the faintest sign of colour.

With regard to the rubies I had expected to find, from my own observation, and subsequently from conversation with the diggers, I soon saw that not only have none been ever found, but none of the signs of the ruby as known at Chantabun or in Burma have been seen. A Siamese official who had been sent here a year ago by the Government to test and report on the place, seeing some small garnets, thought they must be rubies, and thinking to advance himself at head-quarters, bought a very fine Burmese ruby for 70 Rs., and sent it down with his report as having been found in Chieng Kong! From this, of course, very large hopes of the character of the find had been entertained: I fear now he is somewhat in disgrace. Fever, due to the thick forest standing high overhead all around, and the peculiar sickliness always caused by the upturning of new soil, especially in the damp beds of the streams, is very prevalent.

The Burmese houses are very different from the Siamese and Laos —mere bamboo shanties only lifted some 2 feet off the ground, but with all sorts of handy little shelves, window-shutters, doors and lockers, which are generally absent from the others ; and in these, as being easily and quickly constructed, the men always live at their diggings. I do not know the character of the Burmese in this respect at home, but in this country they are always overflowing with friendliness and hospitality to any Englishman; and the headmen at Chieng Kong, especially one by name Monghu, who became a general favourite with my people, and who accompanied us and worked with us everywhere, I can never forget.

The Chow Muang here was lately dead, and just before we left the cremation ceremonies began in the big square before the principal wat. At night the place all round the funeral pyre was lighted with candles; three or four of the head monks were reading in a kind of chant from their Pali manuscripts from the tops of temporary bamboo pulpits, and among the booths standing round; the people squatted in their cloaks, listening to music or hearing descriptive songs and stories, which now and then produced roars of laughter. In the day sports were going on, and there was some very good boxing between the champions of neighbouring villages, who at the end each got three rupees, victor and vanquished alike. The men strip, and their names and the places they hail from are given out. They then salute the master of the ceremonies in the ordinary Laos fashion, touching the ground with their forehead on bended knees, raising the clasped hands to the head, and proceed to business. For some moments they warily watch one another, stepping and dancing round with a good deal of attitudinizing of an alarming description, by the extravagance of which we can generally tell the best man. The blows are rather round-armed, it is true, and kicking is allowed; but it is wonderfully quiet and masterful, and when they warm to it, very hard rounds are fought. The umpires squat round ready to separate the men, call time, and generally see fair play, and at the end of each round the two men squat down, and are offered water out of silver bowls, the bearer respectfully on his knee handing them the ladle. The keenness of the onlookers is tremendous, especially when the men are well matched; but what produced most enthusiasm was a fight between boys of about ten years old. The little fellows showed, I must say, a great deal of pluck and more science than most of us did at that age at school; they kept their tempers well, and at the end of each round their seconds, stalwart fathers and uncles, were beside themselves with delight, stroking their heads and dancing round them with tears of laughter running from their eyes.

There were some sword and sword-and-spear dances by two men in slow time to music, with silver-handled weapons, and accompanied by the gestures in which all these nations take such pleasure.

During the time I was in Chieng Kong district the weather was getting warmer. Up the river we had the minimum 54° three days running, just after sunrise, at which time heavy mists shrouded the river valley, and subsequently 56°, 58°, 60° were the minimum at the same time. The maximum in the shade at the sala or under the coverings in the boats was 91° at 1 p.m.—the average 89°. But in the jungle, where the south-west winds could not reach, the heat was very great, and the sun was very fierce, especially on the great banks of sand, which are so characteristic of the river. The height I make 1250 feet from the sea.

These sands, over which we used to trudge for miles from stream to stream, got so hot after 11 a.m. until about sunset, that the men could not bear walking on them, and took to the water; the glare is tremendous to the eyes. After sunset the rocks retained their heat so that some long-haired Shan dogs we had with us would not lie or walk upon them. There is a great deal of mica, iron pyrites, and magnetic iron ore in these sands; and washing among the bushes, which in many places fringe the higher parts, or some feet down, where a larger gravel lies, one seldom fails to find a small speck or two of gold. The water itself, at this season, rushes through a deep gorge between the rocks and sandbanks, which form its flood-bed, a narrow but very deep column of water, working out for itself, where a bluff rock sends a huge eddy whirling inwards, broad bays often 50 yards across. While the distance between the high-water level on the opposite sides of the valley will be nearly half a mile, the stream itself will often work through its deep channel only 200 yards, and even less in width. The scale of things here is not so large as that

CAMP AT THE FA PA RAPIDS.

below, where the volume of water has increased; but the character of the river is much the same.

The camps we formed on the sand spits, lulled at night by the thunder and roaring echoes from the rapids, were wild and beautiful in the extreme. The jungle, too, was full of night sounds—the bark of the deer or the "peep, peep" of the tiger, of which we often heard three or four at a time; and in the morning their tracks were everywhere upon the sands. It is curious and worth remarking that when one got 4 or 5 miles inland on the left bank no traces of tiger were to be found; while, on the other hand, the elephant tracks became very numerous, and were really useful in threading the jungle; the destruction they work among the trees is wonderful. They seem, however, to avoid the tiger zone near the river, as the tigers in turn prefer the waterside, the latter probably finding greater facility for hunting deer there. There is no doubt that any one who has the inclination, and no work and plenty of time, might have excellent sport by watching for tigers at the drinking-places, which are generally well marked, and are in retired bays, among rocks and bushes.

Bananas and coconuts are very scarce at Chieng Kong; and on the third day after our arrival I had to send the elephants on their

ONE OF OUR ELEPHANTS, WITH HOWDAH ON.

way home, owing to want of wholesome young green food. This all points, with the barrenness we noticed coming across the Nam Sug valley, to a bad soil. They complain that in the hot months, May and April, it is terribly hot and dry, and that "nothing grows;" meaning thereby, no doubt, things do not grow well.

The departure of our elephants was a day of mourning to all of us. The mahouts, very rough Siamese, burnt as black as Hindus, with long locks of hair hanging round their necks, had been very good fellows, and, however long their days, had never complained. All those who have travelled with elephants feel the fascination of the beasts, with their quiet, patient, and sagacious way of treating life; the merry twinkle which sparkles from the small, sharp eyes, and the endless little pranks they are ever ready for; and after some weeks of travelling many a tired and weary day together, this becomes quite an affection; and be sure, if you are fond of an elephant he knows it, and reciprocates it very soon. So we were all very sorry to see them swing off for the south again.

The voyage from Chieng Kong down to Luang Prabang (or Muang Luang, the " great town," as it is usually called) occupies five days if there are no interruptions; the return journey takes from ten to fifteen days against the current, there being a number of bad rapids. The scenery is magnificent, and far surpasses anything I saw on the Mekong below. The river has cut its way almost at right angles to the strike of the rock, a series of schists which appear to have been considerably distorted, until the neighbourhood of the Nam Oo is reached, when the limestones which form the splendid scenery of that river come in. The latter rocks are also seen on the right bank of the big river, where it takes its southerly course south of Ban Soap Ta (one day from Chieng Kong), and there seems to be on the top of a synclinal. They are always characterized in this country by the peculiar dense forests, like the Dong Phya Yen in Lower Siam, the Dong Choi round Chieng Hon, and another one we touched in the valley of the Nam Ngau, east of the Nam Ing, known as Pa Kung Ngau, where the sun never enters owing to the dense foliage, and the elephant tracks form the only paths. We took twelve days going down, making on the way some short expeditions into the country. The inactivity in the boats soon made itself felt, and after five days there were ten men sick out of the twenty Siamese, six with fever and the others with sores, to which they are very liable, any scratch or wound of the slightest description, especially about the feet or legs, always giving rise to them; in fact, I kept one knife on purpose for lancing these things. Wherever we go sick people are brought, and the chief ailments among the Laos were fever, affections of the eyes, and dysentery. The latter is generally taken in hand too late, and ends fatally.

The first day from Chieng Kong we brought up on the south bank, at the mouth of the Nam Ngau I have already mentioned; and I was two nights away with only two or three men visiting some gold washings in the bed of the river. The percentage is extremely

small, and is the same in character though not so rich as in the Mekong sands. The usual small fee of two rupees a year is paid by each man. They work waist deep in the cold rushing stream, and cannot go on for more than ten minutes at a time. A basket is sunk under water with one foot upon it, and the gravel from the bank prized out into it with the usual iron-shod bamboo; it is then lifted out, carried ashore, and washed. This operation, here and throughout the Mekong district, is done by a man standing in the

water, with a wooden tray in front of him, shaped like a Chinaman's peaked hat, the diameter 30 inches, and depth at the centre 5 inches. As it floats on the water, moored by a string to a stone, the basket of gravel is emptied into it, and the larger stones picked out. A rotary motion is given to the pan by the continual shifting of the hands from right to left; at the same time the water is expelled, or dipped up, and sent running round the edge by a depression of the rim being sent round "against the sun," until all the light material is gone. What remains is usually a little magnetic iron ore, with a speck or two of very fine "float" gold for every four baskets of 14 inches diameter and $3\frac{1}{2}$ inches depth. It is then washed carefully into a small oblong box, in which it is carried home and handed over to the women who, I am told (for I never saw it done), use mercury obtained from Chinese merchants for the subsequent freeing of the gold. On the way to Nongkhai we met several gangs of men, generally seven or eight in number, living in their boats and engaged in washing in this way in the sands of the river, in which, according to all I could gather, the gold seems to be redeposited in small quantities by every year's flood season.

What the gold prospects of the country are, there have been no sufficient trials to show, but with the advent of the French on the banks of the river we may soon know something more on this head. The Laos consider they do very well if they get 2 hun per man in a day (5 hun = 1 fuang or $\frac{1}{8}$ tical); but their work is very intermittent, and the search for gold seems to have the proverbial effect upon them, for in several cases I found their assertions were not over-truthful.

Up such rivers as the Nam Beng, Nam Ngau, Nam Oo, and Nam Suung, the gold seems to be in old water deposits which extend beyond the present stream beds, and will probably be found to cover considerable areas in the valley bottoms.

Both calcite and quartz exist in great abundance in the mountain ranges we came in contact with, and to the denudation of these two minerals a great deal of the alluvial gold presumably owes its origin, as well as perhaps from the crystalline limestones. I was, however, unable ever to lay hands on an undoubted gold-bearing vein of either character, nor could I get any information of occurrence of the metal, except in alluvial sands and gravels. Some large nuggets have been found up the Nam Beng and Nam Oo, and up the former river a Chinaman from Luang Prabang had tried systematic working of a kind. After six months' work he lost 200 ticals; and when a Chinaman loses money, especially in a country where money will go so far, the chances are that no one else will make their fortunes. I subsequently found at Pak Beng that the Kache he had employed had swallowed all the decent-sized gold obtained! This is another instance of the difficulties the miner has to meet with in Siam; and with fevers, superstition, robbery, and physical difficulties, the list is a rather alarming one.

This valley of the Nam Ngau is inhabited by people known as Lus. They wear their heads shaved, except for the top tuft, like all the Nan men, with enormously loose and wide blue trousers, often trimmed round the ankle with red; short blue jackets with beads and touches of red; and red, green, or white turbans. They are magnificently made men, with very pleasant countenances, tattooed as usual from knee to waist, but, when clothed, more like the stage-pirate; in fact, a gang of them, with the long dhâps and an old flintlock or two among them, standing chatting, laughing, and smoking their long-stemmed pipes, would make an ideal buccaneer's crew.

At Ban Muang, where we slept each night, the people were the most friendly I had met; some fifty of them came out to greet us on our arrival, and we had an orchestra of four flutes in the evening to play us to sleep. The children and women were extremely pretty. Some distance south of this place the forest already mentioned as Pe Kung Ngau begins. Men travelling in it, and even the people living on its skirts, are subject to a very violent fever, which causes complete prostration in a few hours, and is generally fatal. The face and breast become quite yellow, presumably owing to the stoppage of the bile-duct.

A big dyke has lately been cut from the Nam Ngau to take the water to the eastern side of the valley for purposes of irrigation. Its depth and width are about 10 feet, and it must be some miles long.

THE LEADING MULE.

All the men from the villages turned out to work, and it proved a heavy undertaking. This valley seems to be all under Muang Sa, and Chow Benn Yenn found himself among his friends.

We met another gang of Haws, who made night hideous by discovering the mules had strayed, and every man and boy among them shrieking, howling, beating gongs, and firing guns by way of attracting them back to the camp. It was a pleasant night, with one of my men raving and shouting with fever till dawn.

A DEAD MAN—STERN VIEW.

A DEAD MAN—SIDE VIEW.

At Ban Soap Ta, or Pak Ta, we were in the Province of Luang Prabang. The village is most beautifully situated on the left bank of the river, just below where the wild torrent of the Nam Ta falls into it. There is a regular street all down the village, with deep ditches on each side, between the road and the scattered houses. We met numerous Kache from inland—a perfectly wild people, wearing only the smallest strip of cloth, with a long metal hairpin stuck through the hair rolled up behind, and often a flower in the lobe of the ear. They are short and fleshy, and, though not prepossessing, we subsequently found some of them to be good hard workers, and quiet, simple creatures. The inhabitants of the village were not so smart as our Southern Laos or the Lus we had just left; some of

A HAW—PACKS DISMOUNTED.

them wore slight whiskers, and one or two had thin beards, and there are a good many stout men among them.

We here changed boats, our other craft returning with their crews to Chieng Kong. These boats are mere dug-out canoes, some 60 feet

LAOS BOAT.

long as a rule, with 4 feet beam. They are fitted all along amidships with a light framework of split bamboos, standing up from the gunwale in a barrel shape. On and tied to these are rectangular-shaped pieces of bamboo plaiting, of a primitive character, stuffed with dead leaves, about 8 feet by 6 feet, of which two form the sides, and a third the roof, overlapping them. Two lots together give a good long cabin, and sitting on the light bamboo decking fitted at the level of the gunwale, one has 3 to 4 feet of head room. One's gear goes in underneath, and the men's cooking and camping gear will be stored aft. Two-thirds of the way aft an open space is left, and the decking is discontinued, and here, going through a rapid, bailing is resorted to.

For going down river the most distressingly primitive oars are used, two or three men pulling at them, working in a grommet. The steersman stands aloft astern, with a rudder 6 or 9 feet in length, which he places in a loop on one quarter or the other. To help the speedier turning of the boat in rapids, a long oar is fitted to work athwart-ship out over the stern, and the power of these two is very great, but not too much for the places they are sometimes in. But the most important and ingenious part is the fitting of bundles of

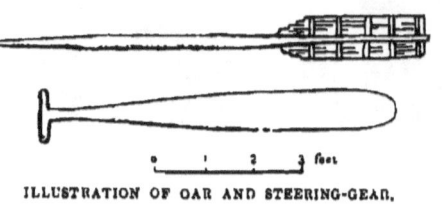

ILLUSTRATION OF OAR AND STEERING-GEAR.

long bamboos round the gunwale outside. Three of these bundles will go to the length of the boat, and they not only give the boat 1½ or 2 feet more beam, and therefore great steadiness, but they act as breakwaters outside her in the rapids, and as air-tight compartments when she is swamped. They are turned up at the ends with the boat's run ; but they hide her very effectually, so that she looks more like a bamboo raft than a boat.

In going up stream, these bamboo bundles are cut adrift, and long bamboos are used for poling from the fore-deck ; the boats winding in and out among the rocks upon the edges, using the swift back currents with such effect that, except on the very rapid parts of the river, the upward journey averages a rate of 3 miles an hour. At the rapids, the boats must be often unloaded and hauled over, this occupying a whole day.

In the flood season, from June to October, the whole river valley is a sea of swift turbid water, often 40 feet above the level of the dry season, as is attested by the hulls of wrecked boats, gigantic tree stems, and water marks, which one sees to that height upon the crags among the sandbanks. Then the boats work their way up among the trees and bushes on the jungle edge. Below Luang Prabang, a double boat is used for going down river, and one gets a wide deck upon it of 10 feet beam ; in these, besides the crew of five men, seven men could live comfortably, while in the single boats, with the crew of four men, four more make rather close quarters.

A great deal of rice goes down the Mekong and Nam Oo for the supply of Luang Prabang from the hills, that town not being

DOUBLE BOAT.

able to supply itself. This rice goes down in tremendously big bamboo rafts, which look like floating villages; they are often some 120 feet long and 30 feet beam. They are allowed to go almost entirely with the current, there being eight or ten long oars rigged out ahead and astern, worked by as many men, for cant- ing the craft in either direction to avoid rocks or eddies. There is a drawing in Mr. Colquhoun's book (which, I believe, is taken from Garnier's work) which gives a good idea of a small one shooting a rapid. They are very un- wieldy, bad to steer, and not too easy to take down these places.

VILLAGE ABOVE PAKU, MEKONG.

Small dug-outs of a pretty shape are used in great numbers for fishing purposes; the boat drifts down broadside to the stream, one man being at either end with a paddle gently working in one hand,

E

the foot often helping, and the other holding a line to the net.   In
these the famous *pla bùk* are caught.   The weight of an average one
is over 130 lbs.   The Laos say they are not common below Nong Khai,
and that they believe them to breed in the retired spots between there

FORTY-FIVE FEET BOAT, NAM OO.

and Luang Prabang.   M. Pavie considers they come all the way from
the sea, but I do not at present know his data; they are certainly
known at Bassac.   The *pla reum* is another large fish, often over

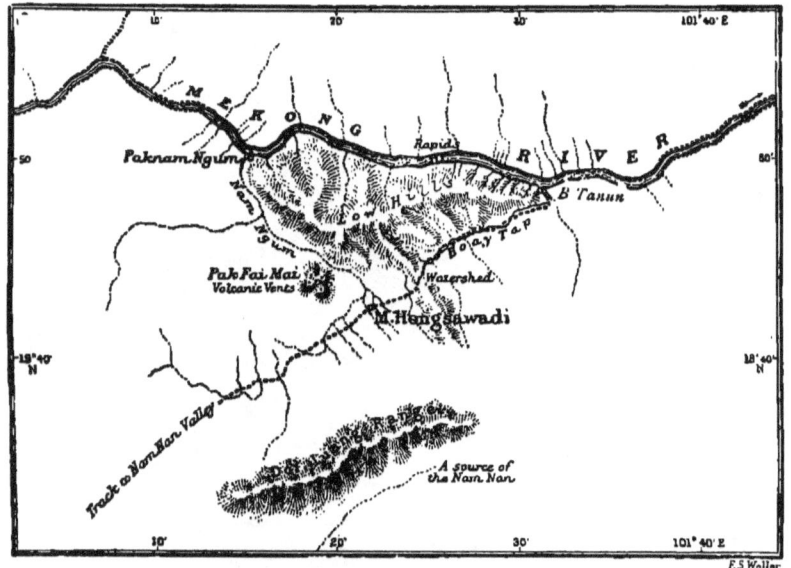

PART OF THE MEKONG.

120 lbs. in weight, which is also known on the Meinam.   Both are
caught extensively, and are sold cut up in steaks in the markets.
     Leaving Pak Ta, the river turns south among a series of schists,
until, after passing the very fine lofty peak of Pa Mon, it resumes its
easterly direction among a lot of wild rapids.   We reached for the

night a temporary village on the north bank, where a number of Laos, engaged in buying rice from the Khache, were encamped. A very wild night of thunderstorms and squalls of wind. The next day was the grandest we had on the Mekong, for the hills close in and form a magnificent gorge, the effect of which was heightened by the wild rain mists which were whirling among the mountains, as the sun rose ahead of us with almost indescribable greens, yellows, and reds. This wonderful scene, and the presence here and there of the little wooden houses, perched high up in their clearings by the Khache

KHACHE HILL CLEARINGS; RAPIDS ABOVE PAK BENG, MEKONG.

where the big trees lay in all directions, or of small villages clustering in apparently inaccessible places, again carried one back to the wilds of Norway. We shot the big rapids of Keng La, and reached Ban Pak Beng that evening. In another day, passing three difficult rapids, Ban Tanun is reached; from which in three days, sleeping at Bans Kokare and Lataen, Muang Luang was in sight ahead at sunset, with the fantastic limestones of the Nam Oo over the stern, and wrapped in thick mists. Our slow speed was due to the constant change of boats and crews.

E 2

From Ban Tanun I made a three-days' tramp south-west over to
the plain of Muang Hongsawadi, to visit the volcanoes marked on
Mr. McCarthy's map.   The track is very rough, up the bed of the
Hoay Tap for some hours, and then over the watershed, from the
summit of which, owing to fires having cleared away the jungle, a
magnificent view was to be had to the south-west over the valley.
The contrast between the rugged uncompromising character of the
Mekong valley behind, and the peaceful expanse of cultivation
nestling below us was delightful.   The villages are all of substantially
built houses ; the people are a smart, tidy, and pleasant race of Laos,

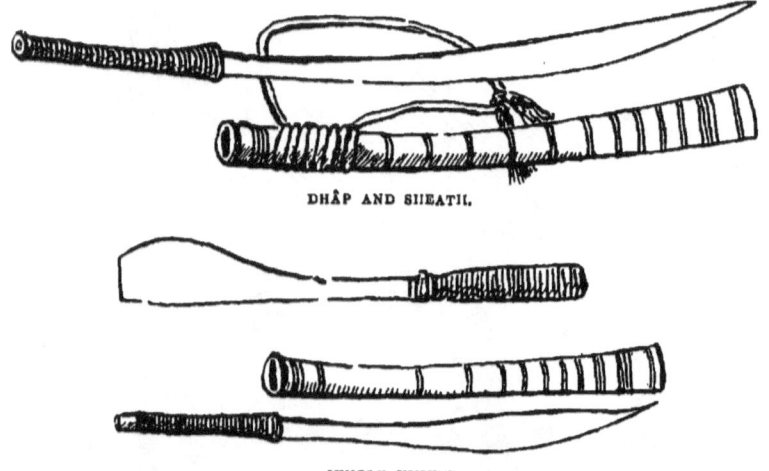

DHÂP AND SHEATH.

JUNGLE KNIVES.

and they are very rich in cattle and elephants ; rice is cheap, and
oranges, pomaloes, and other fruit were plentiful.   The Governor,
who was subject to Luang Prabang, is said to be a hundred and
twenty years of age, and as his house is some miles from the sala,
he sent a message asking me to excuse his calling.

West-north-west about 5 miles is the Pak Fai Mai, as the Laos
call the two volcanic vents which, elevated at not more than 200
feet above the plain, are situated in a thin bamboo jungle.   Each
of the vents is about 200 yards long, sloping slightly in a direction
20° east of south, and 70 to 80 yards wide ; the southerly one is
the least inactive of the two.   Slight smoke rises in several places,
but for the most part one can walk about on the bottom anywhere,

except at the south-eastern end, where there is a series of largish cracks, whence smoke and free sulphurous acid rise in small quantities; here the ground is very hot, and 2 feet in the cracks are red hot, and one can light a bamboo at them. There were traces of the action of sulphuretted hydrogen or of carbonic acid, and the crust of sulphur at the openings may be due to the decomposition of the former gas. I could neither hear nor see of there having been any great activity at any time in the past, but the

MOUTH OF NAM SUUNG, ABOVE LUANG PRABANG.

existence of a present dormant volcanic action is evident. Why this vent has occurred in the position it has is not obvious; there is no apparent line of dislocation, nor has it chosen the valley proper.* In the rains there is, I was told, a good deal of steam rising, as is natural, and more spluttering and activity than we saw. At the northern end there were traces of elephants on the slag (which is everywhere highly coloured from iron chloride); they are proverbially afraid of fire, so it may be inferred that the activity is not great. Southward the vent, which from the slag surface to the top of its sides is not more than 30 feet, is advancing, and the blackened stumps of newly fallen trees and bamboo clumps lie about, with marks of recent falls in the bank.

---

* This valley drains into the Nam Ngum, and so into the Mekong. The big mass of Doi Luang to the south is the division between the Meinam and Mekong drainages here.

The weather was now getting hot, March being the worst month
in this district. Thermometer minimum (for three days south of
Ban Tanun) 72°, maximum in the sala 94°. Distant thunder in
the evenings muttering continually. This weather continued, with
thick haze air, till we reached Luang Prabang. We had fresh south-
westerly winds blowing very hot, and at night rain squalls. Our
first impression of the town was not good; after a long day's pulling,
helping the men, who were very tired with the heat, we got in at
dusk. The temperature ashore, in the streets, or on the sand slope,
was oppressive; but when, after some supper, we went up to call on
Phra Prasada, the Commissioner appointed from Bangkok, and there
enjoyed some real coffee and the luxury of a punkah, in the fine
new Government offices he had just finished building, and heard
the bugles ringing out all round, and the weird march music of

APPROACH TO LUANG PRABANG FROM NORTH.

the kans, which are more played in this province than almost any
other, we forgot the heat in the pleasures of the change of life.

Throughout my stay in this locality, the help we received from
the Commissioner, who is full of energy, was enormous. He has
undoubtedly done a great deal, practically, for the welfare of the
people here, and was most popular; and he has also made extensive
collections of the produce of the province, which will soon be in
Bangkok. He is a man of observation and ideas, absolutely straight,
and without any humbug in his disposition. I was surprised to find
that he could read English well, and talk it moderately, and still
more to find this has all been acquired since he came to the north as
Commissioner seven years ago. This of itself shows an unusual man,
and I record it because it is not often realized that there are such
men among the Siamese. His time was up, and Phya Pechai was
appointed to the post just before I left, and he came south before
the trouble with France reached its climax lately.

PART IV.

LUANG PRABANG (March, 1893).

MAKING expeditions in various directions, Luang Prabang was our head-quarters for about three weeks. Of all the country round, the town itself seems to be the hottest place, and to be away in the jungle was infinitely preferable to staying in the bungalow, where at sunset the thermometer was generally still at 92°. Unlike Nan, Chieng Mai, or Korat, there is no wall around the town, which is the usual collection of substantial teak houses, and large roomy monasteries, of which one-half are in ruins. The latter, however, show signs of some fine gilding and decorative work, and a good deal of architectural effort has been expended upon them. They have been allowed, after the strange custom of the Buddhists, to fall to rack and ruin without an attempt being made to save them; because, one would think, by some strange mistake, the repairing of a monastery makes no merit, though building a brand-new one, however third-rate in style or bad in finish, is one of the highest of merit-making acts.

The chief points one notices in which these wats differ from those in Nan are, the generally low effect, the roofs rising less strikingly than that, for instance, at Muang Sa; the raising at the centre of the roof of what at a distance looks not unlike the lantern of a college hall, which is merely an exterior addition, and does not admit light or air; the small-scale * buildings, of which there are often several in the enclosure, which are best described as being like tiny chapels with vaulted roof, in which, of course, innumerable "phras" stand at the inner end, and which are usually about 14 feet in length, and beautifully proportioned; the small pedestals, which are disposed about on all sides, in a niche in which the small phra is always to be seen; and, finally, the substantial character of the stone enclosure which surrounds the monastery buildings, with often an effective

---

* Called "weehan," or shrine.

porch at the entrance.   In the curves of roof and eaves they show a real artistic sense.   The materials used are brick, covered with stucco, timber, and wood tiles ; and, where an arch is attempted, it is always supported by a horizontal beam in the Chinese fashion, with the

WAT CHIENG TONG.

space above usually filled in, or else a perpendicular goes up from it. It is curious that there are no signs of any knowledge of true arches in these states.

The main feature of the Muang is the central hill known as Kao

PA CHOM SI, LUANG PRABANG.

Chom Pu Si, a bluff of limestone standing up out of the red sandstone plain on which the town is built; its longer axis is parallel with the river, from which it is less than a quarter of a mile distant. On the summit is a small wat, with a lofty pagoda pinnacle visible for miles round; a huge drum hung here is struck every hour by a monk, and its boom rolls down all over the valley.   What with it and the bugles and other wats' gongs, one is never at a loss to know the time. The town is clustered round the hill, and, except on the south, there is water in almost each direction, the Nam Kan coming winding into the big river from the east, just to the north.

The people, among whom slavery was abolished a few years ago by Phya Surasak, who went up as the Siamese general to quiet the Black Flags, are a very independent race, and, possibly mindful of a powerful past, think somewhat of themselves, and do very little manual labour. The men, I regret to own, are very much addicted to opium; stealing is not absolutely unknown, and generally the code of morals is not as severe as in Nan. The

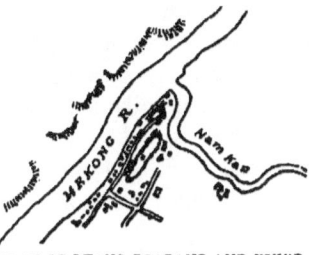

PLAN OF LUANG PRABANG AND RIVER.

women, instead of the timidity and shyness to which we had been accustomed so far (so that, when they could, we always found the women bolt into the jungle at the sight of strangers, or at least retire), showed a very free and easy manner, and are much addicted to giggling and chatter.

The industrious sounds of the foot rice-mills are hardly ever to be heard in the town; and the market, instead of taking place in the early dawn, that the day's work may not be interfered with, lasts roughly from dawn to sunset, with the exception of an hour or two at noon. All down the main street, which runs between the hill and the river, the ladies sit behind their baskets, flirting with the men, who cruise up and down with apparently not much else to do. This market is a very big affair, and besides the usual endless fruit, cigarettes and flowers, there are huge steaks of pla reum, ducks, ducks' and hens' eggs, pigs dead and alive, opium lamps, Japanese matches, needles and pins, cotton, coarse cotton cloth, tobacco, and a fair sprinkling of Manchester goods. Among the people one sees besides the Laos of the place, are Nan Laos, Lus, or Khache, and various hill tribes remarkable for their scanty clothing,[*] Chinese, Shan traders from up the Nam Oo, Haws, and Burmese. At the time of my visit, the French consulate was across on the other side of the river, M. Ducant being in charge there. There is also a French store with all sorts of French goods, connected with the "Syndicat du Haut Laos." These goods I found most unpopular with the people, and when I bought

---

* Such as the Ka Hoks.

one or two things for my men (päs, as they call them, for throwing over the shoulder like a mantle, or for sarongs), they refused to have them, saying the people had told them they were " no good,"—one reason being they would not wash. The imports of this store, brought by boat down the Nam Nua and Nam Oo from Tongking, amounted in February and March, 1893, to 19,841 francs' worth. The Commissioner, and my own observation in part confirmed it, told me that the store has to be heavily subsidized, and is not successful, the goods not being wanted by the Laos, who make their own rough cotton stuffs for hard work, and their own silk finery, and find these more lasting and efficient for the work for which they are wanted. The French-

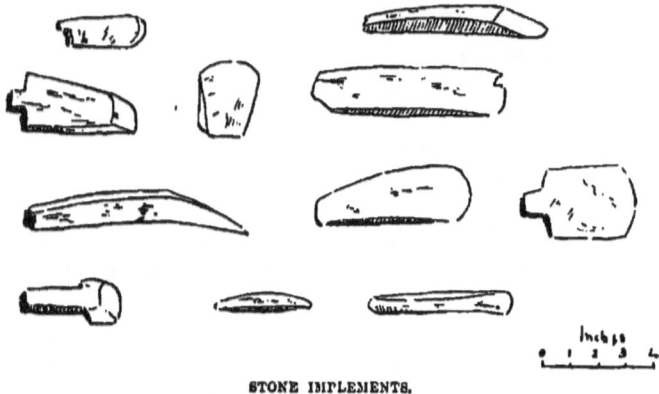

STONE IMPLEMENTS.

men told me they often lose valuable cargoes in the rapids in the Nam Oo. While on this subject, I may say that small tricolours and medals are freely given in all directions to any native who will take them. I found at Nong Khai that the Commissioner had some hundreds of these small flags which had been brought him by the Laos there at different times as having been given them by the Frenchmen, naively remarking that they could "find no use for them," and so they would give them to the Commissioner, if any good to him. These flags are also given largely to the monks, to ornament their wats with, with " Vive la France !" inscribed across them.

Beyond these, I saw no signs of French commerce among the people. The Nam Nua and Nam Oo route over from Jonking, though a rough one, no doubt answers its purpose on the whole, and to M. Pavie, the Minister at Bangkok, who has travelled the country extensively, and has left kindly memories behind him, belongs the credit of it. Another Frenchman who has done good work in the neighbourhood is Dr. Massé, who lately died of fever going down the Mekong. For years he carefully and enthusiastically studied the geology of the district, and he has been able to determine the age of the Luang Prabang series; all his specimens (including some coal and beautifully sharp stone implements) and his papers are, I believe, in M. Pavie's hands, and will prove of enormous interest.

The party at the French Consulate, whether owing to their mode of life, or the climate, did not look well at all; and from the head-aches and fevers which laid hold of the people with me while at M. Luang I am not surprised. In justice to the place, it must be owned, March is the hottest month. I did not see any cases of the famous Luang Prabang fever, which has carried off so many. Like

GOVERNMENT OFFICES, LUANG PRABANG.

that usual in Dong Choi, the temperature rises very fast and very high, and, if fatal, is generally so after two or three days.

There is, or was, a police force in the town recruited from the Laos, but their duties are very light. Fights or quarrelling are unknown, whatever other faults there may be, and the most important part of the police duties is to keep a watch for fires. Only one occurred while we were there, and the promptitude with which the buglers went sounding out the alarm from all the guard-stations and the men turned out was most creditable; luckily there was no wind, and it was got under very quickly.

The head-quarters, as far as the Siamese Government was concerned, were in a newly built set of offices, standing in a large drill-ground; the whole thing was done by the soldiers and the people of the place under Prah Prasadah's orders and watchful eye. It is built of teak, with red-tiled roofing, and consists of a front hall, long offices on both sides, and at the back sleeping-rooms and more offices.   Here, in the evenings, took place regular concerts, to several of which we went for an hour or two.   The people of Luang Prabang are undoubted music-lovers to a high degree, and night after night, after the major and lieutenants had messed, the musicians arrived in the hall, squatted down, and began, sometimes the wailing Laos music, sometimes the quick jig tunes of Siam.   The instruments consisted of two two-stringed violins, a high-pitched flageolet, and one or sometimes two *kans*, a kind of reed-organ carried about by the player, who is the bellows.   Sometimes the bamboo reeds are over 6 feet in length, but they are light; the mouth is applied at a mouthpiece toward the lower end, where the fingers play on each side, there being two sets of reeds side by side.   The instrument is held upright in front or slightly inclined over the shoulder, and the sweetness of the tones is wonderful.   This usually forms a bass, and smaller ones with shorter reeds accompany the voice well.   It would be no exaggeration to say that nearly every household in Luang Prabang possesses one, sometimes two.   A most striking thing it is at night, far into the early hours, to hear the distant kans from all sides playing in the houses, now and then drowned by the nearer approach of one whose master has been out calling late, and goes striding down the road with perhaps three or four more friends in single file behind, playing a march tune with all his lungs like any Highland piper.   One of my pleasant memories of life will ever be those evenings when turning in, after the hot day in the verandah, one listened to the sound of the *kans* passing homeward, and rising and falling on the night-air.   What with the evening bugles, too, and the drum upon the hill, and the cocks and *nok poots*, who never fail to announce the hours 9 p.m., midnight, 3 a.m., and 6 a.m., whether in the jungles or among the dwellings of man, a light sleeper would complain bitterly.

In the concerts at the new offices there were often *kan* solos; while the orchestra, when in full swing, was accompanied by clapping of hands and the tinkle of metal; the songs, albeit curious, were not to me so enjoyable, though very much so to the Laos.   A number of pretty damsels, in their most gorgeous silks, sat round busily chewing betel-nut; these would be asked to give a subject, and one with a good deal of blushing would give in a loud tone her subject.   The orchestra struck up, and the singer had to make the best he could of it on the spot; and judging by the laughter and general approbation after each verse, he was generally successful. But we all failed signally to understand the words—the language here differing very much from that of Nan, of which we had begun to pick up some; while, when sung, it is even more incomprehensible. What with the attractions of music, their love and battle songs, and perhaps other things, the Laos of Luang Prabang keep late hours, and are late to turn out.

The Chow Luang and Chow Huanar, with whom I exchanged visits, are pleasant, open-countenanced men, and after a second visit became quite jovial. The latter helped me a great deal in my work, and I was sorry to say good-bye. Their houses were large teak buildings, but the Chow Luang is building one of brick.

KENG KANG, NAM OO. THE PLUNGE OFF THE LEFT BANK.

Our longest expedition from here was up the Nam Oo, which comes in from the north-east. The scenery of this river is very fine, as all the way from Muang Ngoi, to which we went, it winds through abrupt limestone peaks and ranges, covered with dense forest, and often over-hanging the deep quiet river below. But the rapids scattered along its course are furious, and, owing to the shallow water and innumerable sunken rocks, are very dangerous, while quite a high sea runs in them. They differ from most of the big Mekong rapids in that they are caused by rough sloping bottoms of rock ridges, over which the water tears its way. In the great river the majority of the rapids are simply owing to the narrowing of the channel, with possible big rock obstructions rising out of a depth which, with a 20-fathom line, often gave no bottom (this in low-water season). In these the accelera-tion of speed and commotion are caused by the enormous pressures behind, and the frictions below, and the force of the back eddies, which go tearing in toward any little or big opening in the banks of rock, and come sweeping back again in wave-like rushes or in whirlpools. " Rapid" is often a misnomer; for what with whirlpools, the sudden capricious rushes of water boiling up in a mound of spray, and flowing wildly in apparently any direction but the one by which it will eventually get out, and the great back eddies and counter currents below, the boat, alternately dragged to the right bank, spins round on the edge of a whirlpool, hurries over on a mass of foam to the left side, and there caught and hurried up the side again, or swirled off downwards into another whirlpool, spends several minutes in passing down a hundred yards, though every hand is straining at the oars, and steersman and bow-oar are lugging for dear life to keep her straight, and save her ends from being caught up on the rocks at which she is hurled.

Such are many of the worst of the Mckong rapids, which will

KENG LUANG.

prove too much for any number of steamers, extending often, as they do below Chieng Kan, for miles. Even the great rushes of solid water, and converging lines of breakers of the rapids, where, as in the Keng Luang below Luang Prabang, the already compressed water has to fight its way over a shelving bank of huge shingle, of which each stone is often as big as an average Laos house, will prove easier to navigate. But in the Nam Oo the shallowness of the water is the danger, and there is often, as in Keng Luang two days up, a fall straight over a dioritic ledge of 3 feet. This class of rock it is which forms the rapids, and when the limestone hills retire from the river edge, and low-lying, round-topped hills less densely jungled, come in, one may look out for a rapid and change of formation.

The villages up this river are very poor, except in ducks, which are seen swimming merrily about in all the quiet reaches, and not a few of the rapids. As to buying them, it was almost impossible, though it was the only form of fresh food obtainable. We could hardly get the people to take money, and had to barter, though we were rather short of things ourselves. It is odd how difficult it is to get tea, and as our Bangkok tea had given out, hot water, with some-times a few herbs * picked by Chow Benn Yenn, had to take its place. He also produced a dish of butterflies' bodies one evening with the curry, but they had, to my mind, not much flavour. He also had a weakness for a species of cricket, which he cooked by throwing on the fire, and then devoured. Frogs, too, are eaten by the Laos, they going to the extent of eating the body as well as legs of the *ongan* when the rains begin. The Siamese also eat the *kob*, a small frog, of which the legs are certainly very good ; and when the French gunboats were in Bangkok they were not to be got in the markets for love or money.

Up and down this river a considerable trade in hill rice takes place between the hill villages and Luang Prabang, and we met greater numbers of boats than on the Mekong; they were most of them ascending at the time, with three men, or in the longer craft four, poling. The bamboo is placed against the outside shoulder; the man, facing aft and leaning low, runs the boat up till he reaches the deck-house; he then brings in the pole hand-over-hand until he has it about the middle, and then with the arms straight up above his head, to keep the bamboo over the head of his fellow, goes forward again. This business, continued for hour on hour, is very hard work indeed, as any one who tries it will discover; and the light narrow boat rolls a good deal, making foothold at times very difficult, and no one wearing shoes could stay on board for two minutes.

Going up the rapids is far more dangerous than descending, for the boat has to be poled and often hauled round right angles of rock just outside which a tall hollow sea is jumping in a roaring cataract. If the bows be once caught, away she goes broadside, and nothing will stop her, and all hands at the tow-line go too. It is in this way that all the swampings, as a rule, take place; but, except in Keng Kang, it is seldom that any one is drowned. It is really astonishing at what a rate these fellows run their boats with their poles up the

---

* Termed, when so drunk, "yah," or medicine. It is slightly pungent, and is said to be good in dysentery, and especially for keeping off fever in malarious places.

most difficult places, and then, holding on for a moment under the
lee of a rock, all hands but the steersman go overboard with the rope,
and fight from rock to rock in any speed or depth of current, avoiding
always the big waves.   One soon learns to have a respect for these
exploits, for they mean having one's breath knocked out of one pretty
frequently, and a few good bumps and cuts, which, sad to say, have
a way of leaving some discomfort behind.   But Laos and Siamese
alike are never known to grumble, and after a bout of the kind they
squat down above the rapid, light cigarettes, and laugh with enjoyment.

Fishing on the Nam Oo is very largely practised, the best time
being at the end of the rains, when the fish swarm.   Across the heads
of the rapids are rows of stakes, and every twenty yards will be

ASCENDING KENG LUANG, NAM OO.

a fishing shelter, just above a gap in the stakes, through which the
fish are expected to find their way.   These shelters are light con-
structions, built on groups of stakes, ballasted with stones, and
strongly buttressed on the lower sides.   Notwithstanding these pre-
cautions, however, when the river rose after heavy rains, which had
already (in March) begun higher up, and which delayed us very seriously,
we saw several of these shelters carried away bodily down stream.
On the upper side is a platform, on which the inhabitants (for
they often live, a whole family of them, in these places) may take the
air.   A single bamboo with a handrail forms a connection with the
long line of stakes, by which they may reach the other shelters or get
on shore; but a small dug-out always lies moored below as well.
Step inside the house and all is dark, the light being carefully
excluded, except where it enters through a large hole in the floor;
the *yah kah*, a long jungle grass, with which the houses are always
roofed, is carried on each side right down to the water level, and the
light thus only enters through the water.   Thus every fish for twelve
feet down is clearly seen, and there two men will sit smoking silently

and gazing intently by the hour into the water, every now and then hoisting out a broad dip-net, spread by bamboos, with their prey. A spear is also sometimes used. It is curious to see these people, with wife and family, living on the narrow strip of flooring which goes round the hole—in fact, the latter occupies most of the house; but they seem very comfortable, and smoke, and cook, and feed, and sleep on a strip 3 feet wide with great complacency. The women were very much like the little shy Ka Kaws, and smoked their long pipes and dressed just as elaborately in their dark blue, with the same ornamented head-dresses. However, most of these houses at

FISHING STAKES AND SHELTERS, NAM OO.

this time of year were not inhabited, and I only saw one or two families at home.

Muang Ngoi, at which there was a Siamese military station, is most beautifully situated among precipitous hills; it is one of the prettiest places we saw, well-built, tidy, with a street (as generally in towns in the province of Luang Prabang) running parallel with the river. Immediately over it almost hang the limestones, all round except on the east, up which the people grow their rice in the narrow valley. Up here goes the trade route toward the Black River, and down the track I met coming staggering in under their heavy loads many Ka Kaws—women, girls, and boys. I call them Ka Kaws * for want of a more accurate name; the Siamese called them all Khache,

---

* Probably they were Kuis.

F

or Khamus, which they are not. No one can discriminate among the infinite numbers of these tribes, nor can they do it themselves, except with neighbours of the next valleys.

They wore the prevailing blue; the women's head-gear often a tall, blue cloth, with a little red showing at top, beads and shells. Large rings, of four and more inches in diameter, hang from the ears, of which the lobes are made very big. The weights they carry are enormous; from casually lifting them I should say they were 45 to 50 pounds. The basket is held by a band which passes over the forehead; the result is a stooping gait, the arms being swung across the body, as a sailor's, as they walk or almost jog along. Two or three men usually accompany the carriers; and the latter, even boys and girls, have a terribly worn appearance. Yet greet them with the usual questions: "Where are you bound for?" or "Where are you come from?" "How many days out?" "Are you tired?" etc., and they reply with the merriest laugh and smile, which is almost touching. Their faces have very little of the Laos in them, or of the Chinese or Haws, and are round and kind in expression.

The Siamese troops, only some twenty-five in number, were of fine physique; but it is a fact (not a political statement) that "aggression" and "advance" are utterly contrary to the purposes of the frontier stations kept up by the Siamese Government.

We obtained bananas at one or two places and sugar-cane, and on the way down, as the latter does not grow at Luang Prabang, we loaded our boats deep with the canes, which were, however, short and not very juicy. However, we kept the larder going with cormorants, which were in great numbers both here and down the Mekong.

This brings me to the birds I was able to identify * while in the Mekong drainage. Commonest were these same *cormorants*, which the Laos call "crow duck," owing to their black colour and love for the water. The large cormorant was continually to be seen sitting on isolated rocks, often with his wings hung up to dry, in which position he would suffer us to come very close. The small cormorants were common in flocks, seldom singly, and, on our approach, would dive away out of sight, not one remaining. Not expecting to see them, it was a great pleasure to come across the beautiful little *terns* swooping and rushing over the water. One was either the whiskered tern or

---

* By the help of E. W. Oates' capital handbook to the 'Birds of British Burmah.'

the white-winged black tern—I think probably the latter, as the greyish colour predominated with the dull-red bill and legs. They were generally in back waters and temporary lakes formed in the sandbanks by the fall of the river, and were in flocks. I did not secure any. The black-billed tern—larger than the former, with its easily distinguished orange-yellow bill and red feet, I got a specimen of. They were fairly common, but even in March and April I found no nests.

Of the kingfishers I only saw on the Mekong one or two specimens of the pied bird. Crossing from the Meinam, however, there was a very small one we frequently met in the mountain streams flowing down to that river, which would suddenly fly off up stream with a low whistle. I did not procure any, but from its size it was probably the little three-toed kingfisher. Another we constantly saw perched on a bamboo overhanging the water, or poising in the air, must have been, from its high colouring, the little Indian kingfisher.

Of herons, I saw, and shot, the large white heron (as on the Meinam), singly and in flocks, on the sand-banks; the common heron, generally stalking singly on the sand-spits, and hard to get near; the purple, of which I saw two couples in the lowlands: the little black-billed white heron, in flocks on the flat by the paddy fields; the cattle egret, walking about with the buffaloes, or perched on their backs; and the pond heron, which one would almost stumble upon, so invisible was he on the ground, till away he sped aloft, and then the white wings were clear cut against the blue sky overhead.

Of eagles, there was the osprey, with his white head, hovering after fish, and a larger bird in swamps near the jungle, with white and darting broad tail, and the upper plumage and breast brown, presumably the bar-tailed fishing eagle. I saw some small species too, but never shot any, and, except the black eagle in the forest-covered hills soaring above us on the wing, and a large, slow, sluggish bird, like that we saw on the Meinam, with a hoarse cry (qu. steppe eagle), I seldom got a good view of them.

Adjutants, which they call *nok karien*, I saw in flocks of four, six, or eight in the paddy fields of the Chieng Kong, Nam Ngau, and Khorat plains. They were fairly tame, but with the rifle I could not get nearer than 200 yards; the whistle of a bullet sent them sluggishly flopping their great wings 50 yards or so on, and to follow them was an endless pursuit.

Pea-fowl are very common here and on the Nam Nan.

Often and often, far overhead above the jungle, would come the measured sound which the great pied hornbill makes with each sweep of the wings, an indescribable sound, half a ".whirr " and half the " whistle of a sword swept through the air." They were always in couples, and flew high.

The white ibis, walking about in flocks in shallow water, and the little cotton teal goose, also in flocks, in swampy back waters, who would dive and disappear to a man, I saw several times.

Two specimens of the large grey-headed imperial pigeon, with chestnut back and wing coverts, were shot by my Tuon boatman in the hills above the Meinam. The common "wood pigeon" is seen and heard all through Siam. In the open plains and jungles a dove, of which I shot many for breakfast, was very common; this seems to be the Malay spotted dove.

There are other doves common in different parts of Siam, and wagtails and sandpipers innumerable, but I cannot now name them.

As to the *nok poot*, with his slight crest, dull red-wing coverts and long dark green tail feathers, and his habit of drinking where he finds water, and of running swiftly off into the low jungle, he must, I think, be a pheasant. This is absolutely the commonest bird in the country, and that " poot, poot " sound is never silent for long ; at night I have often heard a chorus of this sound from out the jungle all round, and always at the hours of cock crow, *i.e.* 9 p.m., midnight, 3, and 6 a.m., as mentioned above. The cock in this country is used for a timepiece at night, as well as a fighting champion by day, and not a boat or an ox-cart, caravan, or a cottage in the whole country but has its cock. One result of this cock-fighting mania is very funny: the birds become pets, as dogs and cats do with us, and the small boys go out walking with these things carried lovingly in their arms; you may see them stroking them and looking longingly into their ugly faces as if they found some expression therein. But their end is generally in a curry, and very tough they make it. This form of sport is on the whole most out-rageously general in Siam proper.

The total population of Luang Prabang, including that portion of the province on the right bank, was just over 98,500. In the town itself there cannot be more than about 9000 ; this only includes the Laos proper, and not Lus, Lawas, or Khache.* It is difficult to judge of the town, which straggles along the three or four main roads that have recently been made around the central hill, and far beyond them out into the plain, both inland, up the Nam Kan, and down the Mekong. North of the town are also numbers of fairly large and prosperous villages. The broadening out of the river here, the absence of rapids, and the retirement to the eastward of the hill range, which forms a sort of amphitheatre around the little plain, seems to have attracted settlers from an early time. Still, either owing to the laziness of the inhabitants or, as I think more probably, to the poverty of the soil (which is the same barren red sandstone mentioned above), there is certainly not much cultivation done here or on the other side of the big river, where there is low-lying land behind the small range which immediately abuts on the river there. The jungle, too, is itself very thin and dwarfed. I hardly think laziness will account for this, for peaceful tending of rice crops would be far easier work than poling and struggling up Nam Oo rapids, which is the way the people get their rice at present, going right up into the hills for it. Some really beautiful silver-work is done, but fishing and killing pigs seem to be the chief industry. There is a breed of the finest-shaped and fiercest goats I have ever seen, which wander about the streets and hill, and give the pariah dogs a rough time; but I did not see that any other use was made of them.

The day we left, a letter arrived from the king in Bangkok, and was received in great state by the Chow Luang; it was carried in state down the road with gorgeous umbrellas above and flutes playing before. This was *re* the appointment of Phya Pechai as Commissioner—the last.

The minimum temperature for these three weeks † was 61° up the Nam Oo; the average minimum for ten days up that river, 64°; the average maximum in the deck-house of the boat, 85°. The lowest maximum for any day was 71°, but it was a "saft" day, with a solid deluge for thirty-six hours. (The Laos cannot work in the rain; they shiver to such an extent that the whole boat vibrates, so we spent a day sitting in the boats. In this case I had 3 feet 3 inches

---

* The Khache, or Khamus, are very much confused with the Lawas, and are much like them.

† To the end of March.

head-room, 2 feet 4 inches extreme elbow-room, the boat being only 45 feet long.)

The maximum in Luang Prabang I did not get, being there very little by day; the temperature in the jungle is much lower. Strong, hot winds from south-west and thick haze was the rule except before the storms, when the air became sultry, and then it blew a gale of wind from north-west to north. The rains were beginning. Aneroid, which was unreliable, 28·60 inches to 28·45 before squalls.

The first day out, going south from Luang Prabang, one of our double boats filled and sank, ruining maps, notes, and other things.. We awaited the arrival of another at Pak Si, from whence one of our Laos boatmen had also to be sent back. He had apparently abscess in the liver; I could do nothing for him, and he sank rapidly. The stream Hoay Si, a few miles inland, comes tumbling over a fine fall, where a number of beautiful travartine terraces have been formed below, in which the pools are of intense blue. All the trees, branches, twigs, and leaves within reach of the foam are being encrusted with carbonate of lime, and the effect is very beautiful, with the luxuriant growth around.

Five days brought us to Paklai, whence the trail goes over to M. Pechai on the Meinam. The journey up takes a fortnight, for this long north and south reach is full of serious rapids. Two days and three days below Luang Prabang are the rapids of Keng Seng and Keng Luang. In the former, which tears over a rough bottom, my boat was completely swamped, but was kept afloat by her bamboos. The latter is a very fine sight, and is a narrow contraction, with a rough, inclined bottom; the water tumbles off the bluff domes of the east bank in cascades of foam, and from the west it is driven off in three hollow ridge-like waves. In the centre, at first quietly, and with accelerating pace goes the main mass, getting narrower, until with three huge undulations, which send a boat half her length out of water as she jumps down them, it tears into the embrace of the two raging, broken currents coming off the banks, and there it leaps and foams and thunders, echoing off the big black crystalline rocks from age to age. Many boats are lost here, and just below lay the battered remains of a fine craft of 65 feet, smashed from stem to stern. The Laos show considerable sense in always taking breakfast before they try one of these rapids, however early in the morning.

South of Keng Luang the river bed is narrow, and flows very fast among slate rocks, dipping very steeply (50°, 60°, and upwards), west for many miles, limestone hills lying back some way from the river. These long reaches are very wild, with no sign of man. Birds, crocodiles, and tigers, with occasional pig, " sua pah " or leopard, and deer reign and fight and feed along the jungled banks.

Above Paklai begin the first wooded islands, of which there are many below, and the whole river widens out and hills fall back. Here I was able to get soundings with a 20-fathom line, and above the fine limestone mass which distinguishes Ban Liep, we had 19, 17, 8, 6, 5, 3, and 2 fathoms as the river spread out ; below it it narrowed down a bit, and we had over 10 fathoms most of the way to Paklai, with now and then 6 and 8. Paklai is a pretty little place, and is the official port of departure for the north. There are good salas and elephant stables, and a clearing by the river, a good landing in a creek among the rocks, and plenty of boats and people. But here for the first time we had the abominable little "luep," small black flies, which are a far more irritating torture than mosquitos, and attack one's hands and face by thousands. They are worst just about sunset as a rule, and smoke or a strong breeze are the only things to keep them away, and to sleep in a curtain of linen is absolutely necessary. The rains bring them and most other jungle plagues.

From here the river begins to turn away to the south-east, with quite a new phase of Mekong scenery—placid reaches half a mile wide, with gently sloping banks, the hills low and gentle in their curves, more like some upper reaches in the Meinam, or a bit of Thames. The change was delightful, as it always is, and continued for two days to Chieng Kan, with only one break at Keng Mai, a rapid over a shallow, shelving bank, where the water storms with a bar of white crests right across, like sea breaking on a reef. Decks were cleared and the hands set baling, and we all went through in style, but the cook's boat, which got the least bit athwart the current, was caught in the rough water, and swamped with our rice. The depths down to the town are 1, 2, up to 5 fathoms.

Chieng Kan is built along the southern bank (for here the river begins an east-north-east course), with a fine paddy-growing plain behind it, and is about a mile long, with an indifferent road passing along it. The most remarkable things about the place are the immense numbers of cocoanut palms, and the cheapness of the fruit; [*] the number of Burmese British subjects (who out of the kindness of their hearts supplied one with any amount of provisions); and the fact that the Laos women cut their hair short like the Siamese. The

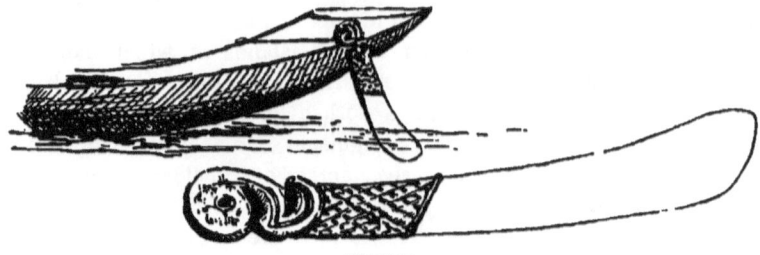

RUDDER.

people are a friendly, pleasant race. A good deal of fishing is done here, and in poling the small craft up stream, a small rudder is used over the outside (in this case starboard) quarter to prevent the boat running round, as also at Luang Prabang and Npngkhai. These

BOATS FISHING.

rudders are fixed, and do their work alone as a rule, but are sometimes in bigger boats fitted with a yoke and long bamboo tiller (as used together in Norwegian boats), the latter reaching to the fore deck. Sometimes in the evening, as the people lie tending their fish-baskets, the boats look, with their up-turned ends and small shelter (in which the man's clothes or his net, with its weights and buoys, may be put) which stands almost amidships, like a distant gondola.

This province, which is under Pechai, is undoubtedly very rich in mineral, but the distances and difficulties of transport are at present against its development. There is a rich, alluvial gold deposit northward, and a variety of ores occur south toward M. Loey, including massive iron-ore beds.

After some stay, we set out with fresh boats and crews, and were five days passing the wild rapids between here and Wieng Chan. The river finds its way among low hills in a narrow, deep channel

---

[*] Eight for a fuang = one-eighth of a tical, or 7½ cents of a dollar. At Pechai we got one for a fuang.

between clay-slate rocks alternating with sandstones and conglo-
merates with a general easterly dip. The rapids are of the whirlpool
and eddy character, and extend for miles on end; the water is in
places confined to a width of 150 feet, and the rushes, boilings,
spinnings, and general deafening pandemonium which results is
astounding; not one place is like another, nor one whirlpool like the
next. Numbers of boats never get through here, as they, in spinning
round in a whirlpool or sudden explosion of water, get their ends
ashore and smashed on the rocks. It was a most tiring time for the
men, deep down in the heat of this great rock ditch, with no wind
to cool the air, and above on either hand a good half-mile of rocks
and vast spaces of sand shimmering in the hot sun.

LAST OF THE HILLS ABOVE WIENG CHAN.

Just above Wieng Chan the hills disappear. The last of them are
a flat-bedded red sandstone, passing into a conglomerate, the huge
slabs lying in rows beside the water. The river opens out between
them into a beautiful wide lake, known as the Hong Pla Buk, from
the numbers of those big fish caught here. The scene on a quiet
evening was beautiful, with the terns dipping and darting about us.
Here in the deep still water, we heard again, as we used to do in
the Meinam, the "talking" of the *Pla liu ma* (dog's-tongue fish)
beneath the boat; it is a grunt similar to that of the gurnard, only
very much louder and more sonorous, and you may hear several at
a time chattering away under you.

Camped on some of these huge sandstone blocks, we had a good
opportunity of watching the polishing power of the wind-swept sand,
which, next to the rushing water, with its enormous burden of sedi-
ment, is the agent by which all the rock surfaces of the Mekong get
the wonderful polish which makes them so peculiar. The exterior
appearances are often entirely deceptive, and the sun glistens off
them as off a looking-glass. Yet the points and pinnacles, especially

among the schists, are terribly sharp, often cutting the feet like knives. The polish the red granite takes just west of this, and the beauty of the veined limestone boulders further north, are a delight to look at.

At Wieng Chan, on the north bank, hardly a hill is in sight; all round plains, bamboos, and palms. The site of the old city, which was destroyed in 1827 by the Siamese for rebellion, is a mass of jungle-covered ruins. The remains of the old brick wall, and of the great

THE RUINS OF WAT PRAKAON, WIENG CHAN.

Wat Prakaon, are very fine; the latter rises from a series of terraces, up which broad flights of steps lead, and is of large proportions. The effect of height is increased by the perpendicular lines of the tall columns, which support the great east and west porticos, and which line the walls along the north and south; the windows between the latter being small, and narrower at top than at the bottom, also

NICHE AND STATUE.

lead the eye up. A second outer row of columns once existed, and the effect must have been very fine. Now the roof is gone, and the whole structure crowned by a dense mass of foliage, as is the case with all the remains of smaller buildings not yet destroyed. One very beautiful little pagoda at the west end is now encased in a magnificent peepul tree which has grown in and around it, and has preserved it in its embrace. There are remains of several deep-water tanks, and the grounds, which were surrounded by a brick wall, must once have been beautiful. But the best thing at Wieng Chan, or the old city, as they call it, is the gem

of a monastery known as Wat Susaket. It is a small building, the
wat itself, of the usual style, with the small lantern rising from.
the central roof, as at Luang Prabang. The walls are very massive,
and, with the height inside, the place was delightfully cool ; all round
the interior from floor to roof the walls are honeycombed with small
niches in rows, in which stand the little gilt "prahs," looking out
imperturbably, generally about 8 inches in height.

Round this building outside runs a rectangular cloister, which
faces inwards, and here, at one time, the monks were living among
the statues which stand round the walls, many of these 3 and more

SOUTH-WEST ANGLE, WAT SUSAKET, WIENG CHAN.

feet high, while the walls too are ornamented with niches similar to
those inside the main building. In the centre of each side there is a
gateway surmounted by a gable, there being also similar ornaments at
each corner. The beauty and the retired air of the court inside could
not be surpassed, and the effect of the green grass, the white walls,
the low-reaching red-tiled roofs, and the deep shadows is charming ;
there is nothing flat, nothing vulgarly gaudy, and very little that is
out of repair. And here, as is most noticeable in the remains of
the other buildings about, the proportions are perfect. In this the
ruined remains of Wieng Chan surpass all the other buildings I
have seen in Siam, and bear witness to a true artistic sense in the
builders. Though the old city is not inhabited, and the site thereof
seems under a curse, the villages along the bank of the river, both
above and below, have a flourishing appearance, and the paths along
the river, with their cool shade, were full of people.

Leaving Wieng Chan, we had our last and most curious experience of the Meinam Kong and its wanton ways. A vast mass of heavy thunderclouds lay to the east, south-east, and south, and into this, as happens in the rainy season, a strong draught of air, first from south-west, then west, and then north-west, was blowing. This began to freshen, and with two square sails I got rigged to my ship we made very good way, until it began blowing really hard and a sea got up, the water being here over half a mile in width, with 2, 3, and 5-fathom soundings; we then had to strike sail, while astern a vast cloud of sand, twigs, leaves, and even pebbles, came sweeping along with a roar. The other three boats were, when we saw them last, just broaching to, all close together. The Laos, who face rapids or elephants with composure, quite lost their heads, and the only use to be made of them was to set them to hang on to the deck-house, which was being carried out of the ship. She tried very hard to swamp herself, for when the squall came up the strength was terrific, and the seas hollow and breaking solidly. However, by keeping her stern to it, we shot on through the thick darkness, frequently belaboured with missiles, and after a great deal of difficulty in weathering a lee shore we got round a point and brought up, after two rattan ropes had been carried away. Meantime many dug-outs passed us waterlogged and adrift, and when at last the wind got to the north and fell not a boat was in sight. Except our own, every other craft in the river had been swamped, including our other three boats, which were carried broadside into the lee shore we had got round, and had a handsome battering. Everything in them was full of water, while the men escaped and sat on shore till it was all over, and when they arrived at Ban Bar, where we lay for the night, they did not seem to have enjoyed the fun at all.

This village is more Siamese than Laos in appearance; there are numbers of Chinamen of unprepossessing appearance and manners, who kept shops and pariahs. The latter was a nuisance we had been comparatively free from ; in fact, on the upper river, at Chieng Kong, there were very decent breeds to be seen, and Chow Benn Yenn got from one of his villages a beautiful black-and-tan collie, exactly like a good specimen at home, with the exception that he had a short tail like a manx cat. It was a beautiful dog and a capital sporting animal. The long black-haired and black-tongued "Chow" dog we saw several times, and also small, brown, long-haired animals with high, curled tails. A peculiarity about these dogs was that, being accustomed to the Laos *kao neo*, when we got back to Siam and *kao chow* (the ordinary rice), they would have none of it.

The next day we reached Nongkhai, and were very cordially welcomed by Krom Prachak, a brother of the king, who is Commissioner. The town owes its existence to the fall of Wieng Chan, and is scattered along the south bank ; there is a considerable number of Chinamen keeping shops here, and to them and its character as the official centre, it owes its importance. The houses extend all along the river-side for a mile and a half, mostly well shaded by areca and coconut palms. Here once more, on the great plain lying to the south, we saw the tall, gaunt sugar palms standing against the sky, and again saw the *kiens*, or ox-carts, with their long, black hoods, wending their slow way in single file, the groaning, grunting, and shrieking, which accompanies their every movement and jerk, coming slowly down the wind. Here once more, sad to say, we came across a character most of us have known in Siam—the *kamoë*, or thief— and we hadn't been an hour in the place before he had begun work. Here, too, we again heard the horrid sound of chains, dragged along the hot, dusty road by wretched, emaciated creatures carrying water —hardly strong enough to lift the chains at their ankles. And here, again, were, among the decent houses, dirty, squalid cottages and drunkenness. The fact is, the cattle-driving people of the plains become by their occupation different in character to the mountaineers ; it was ·very noticeable, striking right upon them here, how much more stolid and less expressive their faces are, how black and muddy —or dusty if the rain keeps off—they become in their long, slow rides upon their carts, and, in general, how like their own sleepy, blinking buffaloes they become—as, too, one may see in the great plains of India. The circumstances and conditions of life are all different; and drinking slow-running mud, which they euphemistically call water, sloshing laboriously through seas of reeking bog and swamp, and enduring the tormenting bites of innumerable huge flies, which attack elephants, buffaloes, oxen, horses, and men indiscriminately, but untiringly, must result in a differently developed man from that built up by mountain marches, high aloft on dry hillsides or deep down in cold stream beds, leaping from rock to stone or plunging into the rushing water, where life is a perfect fight. Not that the plains are always so disagreeable; given the dry, cool months of December and January, travelling in them becomes a luxury; but there is never the same exhilarating air or the same pure water.

The Commissioner's house is at the western end of the town, surrounded by the sheds of the military detachment. At the back a very pretty garden is being made; and this and a new straight road, inland of the present street and parallel with it, are the works of construction on hand. The ground on each side of the new road—which, by its unlovely straightness, carried one far away to similar ugliness in civilized lands, and was the only unnatural thing we saw —is being eagerly applied for by the Chinese; but a great drawback must for some time be the absence of shade. The river is undoubtedly cutting into the soft laterite bank here, and in a few years the old site will go down with a run.

Prince Prachak is a reformer; he is very keen in "reforming the Laos," but is grieved to find they don't want to be reformed. He says—what is very true—that their work is always desultory (one month they plant rice, another they go fishing, another they wash gold in the sands), and that they will not settle down into trades. They prefer, too, to play music on their kans in the evenings to doing more useful things, and are, in fact, lazy. But I fear it is not surprising, and that it will be some time before the Laos take to trades.

The Chinese shopkeepers import their goods from Bangkok through Khorat, and the journey, in the matter of shoes or felt hats from London, increases the price about one *salung* at the first place, and two by the time they reach Nongkhai. They show for sale calico goods of all colours and patterns (as one sees in Bangkok for "pan-

BELL.

ungs," "pahs," etc.), shoes, sandals, belts, pots and pans, matches, Chinese umbrellas, and tea-pots, the first mostly English, and as they sell these well, they tell you with a grin they soon make their fortunes and retire.

The wats are wretched little places, ill built and ill kept, the most interesting thing being the bell of the principal wat, which is a huge hollowed timber, some 3 feet in diameter and 7 feet high, hung to a crossbar at the top. Struck end on with a stout pole, the sound is deep and sonorous. This form, but usually smaller, is often used in Siam, and for attaching to the necks of elephants or oxen (which invariably have a bell), there are clappers hung on a string on each side, which keep up a continual tinkle. Fixed on a bent bamboo, the same form of bell is used by fishermen on the shore end of their set lines to give warning of a big fish or other disturbance. There is always a slit up, about a quarter of the way, slightly wider at the top, on each side.

The weather from the time we left Luang Prabang to the time we reached Nongkhai had the unsettled character of the beginning of the rains, though it was only April month. South-westerly winds and haze by day, low heavy clouds in the evenings, and thunder-storms of great violence, with strong squalls of wind shifting round

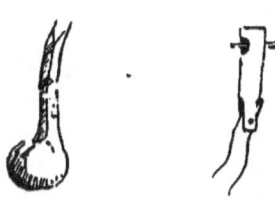

BELL-CLAPPER AND JOINT.

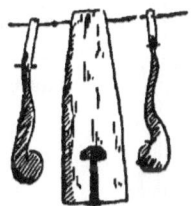

BAMBOO BELL.

by west and north-west to north at night, making sleep impossible while they lasted, and generally driving into the boats everywhere. The lowest and highest readings of the thermometer were, on the same day when we arrived at Chieng Kan, after some heavy storms, 63° Fahr. at sunrise, 104° at 2 p.m. in the boats. For the rest of the time, the average minimum was 72°, generally half an hour before sunrise. The average maximum in the shade, 92° (in the boats). In the shady sala, on the tree-covered bank at Nongkhai, we never had over 89°, and, whether owing to the advent of the rains or not I do not know, it was much cooler and pleasanter than Luang Prabang had been, and all our sick men, with one or two exceptions, mended entirely; while at the former place (as too in the case of Mr. Archer's party) every one had had turns of fever or bad headaches.

The coinage here was once more the tical, with only an occasional rupee. At Luang Prabang the two, with their small silver sub-divisions, are both taken; but in Nan no Siamese money would pass, strings of areca nut being used for small change, as cowries are at Luang Prabang.

Note on the " Kan."

The Kan, the reed-organ used so much among the northern Lao tribes, is remarkable for the sweetness of its tones, and the fact that the intervals of the notes are correct according to our musical ideas, and have a true key-note, the pitch of the instrument depending on its length.

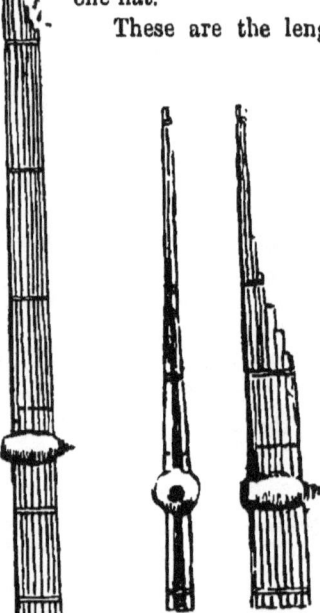

Thus the five-sok kan (9 feet 4 inches long) is in the key of G—one sharp.

The four-sok kan (6 feet 8 inches) in the key of D— two sharps.

The two-sok kan (3 feet 4 inches) in the key of F— one flat.

These are the lengths most usual, but six soks is sometimes used; it possesses very fine low tones, but requires powerful lungs, although the notes are produced by inspiration and respiration.

The number of reeds never exceeds fourteen, and the arrangement of notes is as follows, numbering the reeds in couples from the mouth of the little air-chamber:—The two reeds, 1, are played with the thumb; left 1 being the key-note; right 2 being the lower octave of the same. The octave thus goes from right 2, to 3, 4, 5 and 6 left (or right 3, which is the same) on to right 4, 5, and back to the thumb note on left 1.

FOUR-SOK KAN   TWO-SOK KAN.
(1 INCH TO 2 FEET).

Below the key-note right 2 come left 2 and right 1, and above the upper key-note, right 6 and 7 and left 7; thus, in the D kan of four soks, we get—

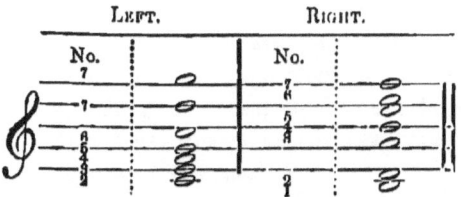

There are no sharps or flats possible, and only half filling the holes, as in a fife, will not produce them, the note being got by the vibration of small tongues of metal fitted in the side of the reed. Hence, possibly, the epithet "monotonous," which has been generally given them; and hence the fact that a good player generally has more than one. Their playing is very fast and effective, but is at first hard to follow or properly understand. The mouth-piece is made of the fruit of the *mai lamut*, and being very hard, takes a lot of work in being hollowed out, and will receive a good polish outside; two parallel slits are cut along the top and bottom, and the two rows of bamboos fitted in, and the whole made airtight with beeswax. In case of damage to one of the reeds, it is quite simple to undo the grass bands which are put round at intervals, to remove the beeswax, and take out the reed; often a gentle flick on the reed will set the metal tongue vibrating again when momentarily out of order. The reeds, by being put over the fire, are often very prettily marked.

AIR-CHAMBER.

They can hardly be obtained in Siam, except where Laos are situated.

The Wieng Chan men, who are all over the country since the city was destroyed and they were sent south, are the best makers and players, and a few colonies of them are to be met with in the neighbourhood of Bangkok. This fact of their love for this highest of Indo-Chinese instruments, coupled with the fine remains of the old city, certainly support the idea that at Wieng Chan there was civilization and taste ahead of those of the surrounding places.

With regard to the music, it is impossible, without a long study of it, to say more than that they are very fond of the minor, that they use the octaves very much in playing, that the key-note may often be heard down for a long time, and the time is generally a

G

rapid horse's trot, or quick march. At Nongkhai, I heard two men play a most beautiful and stately march which made one's flesh creep; it was all in the major, and in some parts irresistibly reminded one of the famous march in *Saul*. One of these was a six-sok instrument, and the effect surpassed anything I've heard in the country. They were on their way to a marriage-festival when I met them in the road; they had no fiddles or flutes with them, and were followed by a number of people marching with them to their airs. They willingly stopped, squatted down, and gave us half an hour's concert in the shade.

PART V.

NONGKHAI TO KHORAT AND BANGKOK (*April and May,* 1893).

FROM Nongkhai we left in regular rainy weather for Khorat, with 14 " kiens " or ox-carts, there being two oxen and a driver to each. Twelve of these are about equal in carrying capacity to sixteen elephants as loaded for hilly country—two extra we had for sick men, of whom we still had two unable to walk ; and these two, more-over, were the best protected with charms of all the men with us. These charms were small wooden *prahs,* very roughly cut, which they sew up in a bag of calico and wear round the neck and arm. No amount of chaff will persuade them that these things will not protect them from falling trees, and *dhâp* (or sword) cuts, as well as the *Pi* of the forest or river. Another danger from which they declared these things protected the whole party, were the mermaids in the Mekong. Against these creatures I was constantly warned when having a swim, especially above Luang Prabang; they de-scribed them as the "women of the water," who would drag a man down and drown him. Where could this notion have come from, so singularly like our own stories ? * South of Luang Prabang, one heard very little of these damsels, and much more of the *pla bûk.* On one occasion I pitched one of these charms overboard, and the owner, who was sick, promptly got well next day, to his no small astonishment.

Following the telegraph line, the great trail to Khorat is 211 miles or so, but *detours* have often to be made in search of villages which are generally off the main track some little distance, and this is necessary for commissariat purposes. For traders, the journey generally occupies 16 to 21 days, according to the condition of the oxen and state of the weather. When it rains, no advance is possible, as, unlike the buffaloes, the oxen cannot work in rain, and

---

* It no doubt primarily arises from the danger and strength of the eddies.

hate it, and seem to lose all their pluck; besides which, the yoke working on the damp neck tends to produce bad sores.

The *kiens*, of which we frequently met long caravans, are the ships of this desert—for such this plain is often for days at a time. Nothing but wood is used in the construction, as the bumping and straining is too great for any metal fastenings. The body of the carriage proper is very light, like a cariole in shape; the pole to which the yoke is attached spreading and passing along to the rear underneath. The wheels, which are very broad, and the heaviest things in the whole, turn on an axletree of hard wood (*Mai Kabao*, sometimes *Mai Deng*), which is fitted in a socket of solid wood under the car, at the inner end, and at the outer to an "outrigger," which is lashed at its end to cross-pieces firmly placed at right angles at the front and rear ends of

KIEN.

the car. Thus the weight is distributed on many points; a few ready-cut extra pieces of mai kabao are taken, and when with a lurch and a dive one of the axletrees gives way, the "outrigger" is unlashed at one end, and pulled outwards till the axletree comes out of its socket; it is then pulled out of the wheel, and a new one fitted in in a quarter of an hour. Similarly, lashings may now and then give way, but a new one is put on in five minutes. Over all a closely plaited cover is fitted, with a long peak forward, reaching out over where the driver sits on the pole; and in this a man may sleep protected from sun and rain. The length of the car is about 7 feet and 3 feet wide. Travelling in it is only possible to a person who is accustomed to it, the jerking being so tremendous. If there were roads it would be possible with some degree of comfort, and, though dusty, they keep cool inside.

The oxen are capital animals for their purpose, and when tired and hungry can be turned loose with a certainty that in a quarter of an hour they will have satisfied themselves; the moment they have had enough, even of the rankest grass, they are ready to go on; their patience and perseverance, even in the worst swamps, pestered with flies and leeches, is wonderful. A frisky one, however, can do no end of damage, and can kick and plunge and drag the *kien*, even when loaded, at a gallop over any kind of country, and even the rein in his nose will not hold him. On occasions of this sort, some damage is often done to the cart, and delay occasioned. Their kick is very quick, and pretty severe. They are always used by the Laos, though seldom used by the Siamese of the south.

The buffalo, which wallows in the water all over Siam, is generally kept for working the rice or sugar mills, and is only occasionally used by the Laos in a larger cart of the same kind; but he is very surly, wilful, and erratic. Large droves of them are taken south from the Nongkhai neighbourhood, where their price is 12 to 15 ticals, to Khorat, where their price is double; the demand for them and oxen being very great in that neighbourhood. The best ponies come from the neighbourhood of M. Chulabut, but they are also very cheap round Khorat. At the former place, I saw some capital beasts, and from that neighbourhood and the south at Pachim the cheapest ponies are obtainable. Prices for a good carrier range from 50 to 100 ticals, though an average pony of three years old, which will carry one fairly well in ordinary jungle work, may be obtained for 35 to 40 ticals. They are very small, and have a peculiar fast trot, which makes rising in the saddle impossible; the Siamese or Laos always sit tight in the saddle, legs almost touching the ground. At Chulabut, I saw a small creature of ten hands which was very wild, and the owner wanted to get rid of him for 8 ticals; he was a wonderful little beast, and very fiery. Another I was offered for 20, and another for 30; but they would be useless for Europeans.

For two days we travelled fairly easily, leaving the slight cultivation near Nongkhai, and travelling through low, shadeless jungles, passing here and there salt-boiling pans, at which the most work is done after the rainy season, there being at other times no water. The salt covers the ground in an efflorescence, and that produced by the villages is coarse and bitter. The soil in the jungles is sandy, there being gentle undulations on the northern side, on which the sand is deepest; on the southern the trail going over rough laterite. In the depressions occur the *nongs*, or swamps, of which the plateau is full, and which in the wet weather, with their mud and deep water, make travelling almost (and in most places quite) impossible. In the neighbourhood of the main streams, which all run from west to east to the Mekong, villages are established, and the scrub jungle gives place to the welcome bamboo clumps and the high betel and coconut palms, which, like church spires at home, announce to the traveller far away that he is approaching the habitations of men.

The absence of good water, and the change in it, made several of the men very ill, and on the third morning I found one of the original invalids, who had had a lot of fever on the Mekong, had every sign of abscess in the liver. I knew at Khorat there might be a doctor, so took two men with me, with three *kiens* and their drivers, pushed on, and arrived in nine days. The man recovered there, and was well enough to go on with us from Khorat afterwards.

I had heard so much of the goodness of the trail following the telegraphic clearing all the way, and of the bridges and salas, that I was very much surprised at the reality. It was the worst track we had followed, and there were only two salas which had roofs on them the whole way, one having been put up at his own expense by an officer at Chulabut. The rest were blackened stumps, and solitary corner posts, from which every bit of roofing and flooring had been removed; two of these having just roof enough to keep out the dew, but no more. Cheerless places enough to reach an hour after sunset, after having marched all day in the scorching morning sun and the deluge of rain which came every afternoon and continued most of the night.

However, though after the Hill Laos, their "white-bellied" brethren of the plains were in some ways disappointing, I am bound to say that the men who were driving our kiens behaved splendidly; one of them was formerly a sergeant, and knew his drill and the English words of command once used in the Siamese army well. He was the lightest and warmest-hearted man I ever travelled with, besides being, what is not too common in the East, a really smart man. He was the headman of our caravan, and I had told him that I must get on as fast as was possible to Khorat, and he must help; he jumped at it. I asked him how quick we could do it from Song Prue. "Ten days." I told him, in that case we could also do it in nine, and he was delighted, and used to turn us out at four o'clock with his loud *sawang lëo* (daylight come), long before there was a sign of light, and then laugh and say, " Nine days, master." And so, whatever the weather, however long we stood waiting in the rain for the oxen to rest their necks before goading them on again, none of these men with me ever thought of growling; and the Siamese were the same. The pony I had brought on soon got a sore back, so there was not much riding, except when it came to swimming a stream.

The bridges were three in number only; one was possible, the other two were unfortunately not connected with the southern bank, so that in one case at Meinam Chieng Kun, the waggons, after having the oxen taken out, are hauled over the loose flooring of the bridge and dropped at the end into five feet of mud and water; in the other every one avoids the bridge altogether. Now, at very small expense, for the labour can be obtained for the necessary time from the neighbourhood, good bridges might be erected all along this route; as it is, the journey, as soon as the waters begin to rise, is of the most difficult and arduous kind for all these caravans.

Krom Prachak is very eager for a light railway from Khorat to Nongkhai. At least years must elapse before it can be done, but in three months a good cart-road might be made, pile bridges put up, and salas repaired; then it would be possible to judge of the chances of such a railway, and the groundwork for it would be already laid. At the present moment this undulating country, which should be easy to travel, is worse provided with communications than the greater part of the hill villages in Nan, and infinitely worse provided with shelter than in the most out-of-the-way mountain valleys north. Yet, wherever we went, the same kindly Laos welcome was given us, except in places where there were Siamese settlements near by, and friction had probably occurred among the petty officials.

Some of the villages, to which we went slightly off the trail, such as Ban Tum, between the Nam Puang and Meinam Si (both big streams, very deep and swift when the water rises, flowing through extensive paddy plains and swamps), Chulabut one day south of it, and Ban Bodibun just north of Khorat, were perfect gem villages, rich in palms, rice, and cattle, with kindly people, who did all in their power to overfeed us before we started. At the former places, where there were Siamese officials, everything was very neat, and the relations between them and the Laos seemed to be most happy. This is, naturally, not always the case; but I am bound to say that, wherever the official is one of some standing, this state of things is the usual one. Cultivation goes on round the villages; but as soon as one gets a couple of miles away, the sandy jungle or the *nongs* resume their sway. The latter are the most peculiar feature of the region, and cover a vast area, which is larger to the eastward. Some of them are merely small swamps, with shallow water and long reeds, extending over a surface of one or two square miles; others, again, are extensive areas, in which water and reeds are the only object the eye meets for miles, with here and there a little green island, where trees exist, and, in the distance, the low, long, green line of the jungle along its edge; an ideal home for the various herons, and other long-legged waders, but, alas! also tenanted by leeches and by flies, who attacked us all. The poor little oxen, at the end of a few miles, especially if the sun came out for a little in the burning way it does between rains, were covered with clouds of the latter, their necks and nose, humps and legs, smeared with blood. No resting is possible, for every moment a stop is made the deeper everything sinks into the mud; so it is plunging and struggling to the next little island, where we would stop and cook breakfast with a score of other weary mud-bespattered carts. Besides these, we also met some pack-oxen going north to get salt; but as the water was out everywhere, they would have to wait before returning south. One may roughly say that the salt efflorescence occupies the low grounds, between the slightly higher laterite jungle ridges, which are yet just higher than the surface of the *nongs*. The villages in the neighbourhood are generally wretchedly dirty and untidy in appearance; the growth is only stunted bamboo, and the whole place uninviting enough.

The cold weather, with its advantages of dryness and absence of insects, has also the disadvantage that water is very scarce. When we crossed, the whole low-lying area may be said to have been under water, but water of such a description that it was only here and there that it was fit for man to drink; while in the sandy forests the water, all perforating through, drained off at once, and the lower ends of the track, where it began to rise toward the ridges, were, on the other hand, lakes of mud. Thus, between endless seas of bad water and long miles of sand, the water question remains almost as serious in the rains as in the dry weather. The villages, as a rule, have a well, and the water from the wells is fair.

The method of travelling usually adopted with the *kiens* is an early start at dawn, and a journey of some 300 sen (7½ miles), when a stop is made to feed man and beast; and, if going easily, a start will not be made until 3 or 4 p.m., when another 300 sen will be done before night—a speed of 15 miles a day, occupying about 6 hours, at about 100 sen (2½ miles) an hour. This is very fair work for ox-carts over a well-worn track, which is, of course, much rougher and harder to travel than the jungle itself, the ruts spreading wide for a breadth of 30 yards or so, and being of any depth that a *kien* wheel can dig to. But this exceeds the average.

Being in a hurry, we did about 21 miles a day for nine days, but had three relays of oxen. This involved—at about 8 to 10 hours' travelling by day, with the delays necessary to get new oxen, two half-day rests, and fording the streams (where the waggons had to be often carried over on the men's shoulders)—a good deal of night travelling, which in rain, and heavy trails full of pitfalls, does not commend itself as a rule. It will be seen, therefore, that the rate of travelling is slow, and would be sufficiently increased for all present purposes by improvements in the trail, and at the crossing of the rivers. Men who are walking have, of course, the advantage, and sometimes do 24 or 25 miles a day with their packs. The latter are usually carried on the two ends of a long bamboo, and are fitted with legs below, so that, stooping down, the weight is at once taken off the shoulder. When he wants to rest, out of one of his panniers the man takes his mat to sit on, and lays it between the panniers, and over the pole above he places the *bai larn* (a covering of palm leaves sewn together, some 6 feet by 5 feet) to keep off the sun or rain, and this is his house while he is on his journey. *Dhâps* are rare here, and heavy knives are used for cutting down jungle to place round at night, or leaves to place under the bed. From travellers of this sort, going south, we often bought wild honey, in long bamboos—2 feet of a 3-inch diameter bamboo selling for a fuang. They sometimes set traps, and are successful in catching rabbits.

There are a few deer to be heard, and tigers are rare, except round Chulabut, where a man was killed after we had left, the day the main body arrived there.

We picked up a rather curious fellow-traveller when about six

days from Khorat, and he accompanied us to within a day of the town.
This was a rather decent-looking pariah dog, of quite remarkable
character. Unasked he joined us, and trotting often with me in
advance, or half a mile ahead, or right behind us all, his short sharp
bark might be continually heard in the jungle to right or left as
he hunted his breakfast. Of what this consisted I never knew,
but he kept himself in fair condition, for he got very little from us,
poor thing, as we did not want to encourage him; he got more
kicks than ha'pence. But he stuck to us, and even when we over-
hauled other parties going south, instead of stopping and going

THE NORTH GATE AND NAM NUN, KHORAT.

leisurely with them, he always came on with us. He was evidently
accustomed to travelling, and knew the trail, for he was often absent
half a day, but would turn up in the evening, and lie near us for
the night. When we halted, and placed the waggons round us, and
the men put their sleeping-mats underneath them; he would come
as near the fire as he dare to get dry and warm. Sometimes in the
heat at noon, when the sun had been blazing upon us in the sandy
jungle, we would come upon him lying in a *nong*, with only his eyes
nose, and mouth out of water; while in the rain he plodded stolidly
along, and would sit down and wag his dripping tail when he saw
we were going to camp.

At length we saw the high line of foliage topped by palms which marks Khorat, and through seas of mud, arrived on the bank of the Nam Nun, which flows along the northern wall of the city. Across the ford were groups of waggons encamped to the number of about fifty, and by an old wat under the shade a busy market was going on. The Commissioner here, Phra Prasadit, is the same stamp of man as the Commissioner at Luang Prabang: one of those energetic, warm-hearted, and cheerful men who make such excellent governors. He was kindness itself to us, and all the men under him reflected it. In Siam, where every man has in proportion to his importance numbers of others attached to him by a kind of feudal relationship, and where his office clerks and his lieutenants all have a personal connection with him, and almost form part of his family, the influence which can be exerted is unbounded, and by the expressions of face of the inferiors the superior may be judged. Moreover, the Commissioner in Khorat is a man of ideas, has been in Europe, and has a good knowledge of English and a fair knowledge of French, and in all political questions in these countries he takes a great interest; and thus his company was very pleasant.

The centre of the town we found not yet recovered from an extensive fire; all round the four sides run the lofty red-brick walls, with gates in the centre of each side, protected by round towers at the flanks, in which laterite blocks have been extensively used. The whole is much dilapidated and overgrown, and the moat outside has become nearly filled up. The Commissioner had then 3000 men at work clearing it out again. This will probably enormously benefit the town, which at present may be described as an accumulation of houses, mainly in ruins, jungle patches, and swamps, on every side of which rises the great mound on which the walls stand, and which effectually shuts in every drop of water, and in the rains transforms the whole area into a lake. With openings made under the walls to drain off the water into the moat, and with a raising of the level inside, an enormous improvement will be effected. As the town stands well on a slight rise above the plain level, and is surrounded with similar ridges covered only with beautiful turf going miles towards the south, south-west, and south-east, it may become a healthy and attractive place. The plain around is dotted with villages; for many miles the soil certainly produces a fine clean rice and abundance of fruit. Going out in the morning along any of the great trails to the west, north, or east, one passes among crowds of camped *kiens*, and among villages and markets, the latter always held along one side of the road. At the time we were there mangoes were in full swing, and all the women's baskets full of them, bananas, coconuts, ready-rolled cigarettes, brown cakes of palm sugar of an excellent quality, and very often the fruit of the sugar palm, which is very much enjoyed. To the south and west the trails are really like beautiful roads, for they go through a pretty red sand soil, leading to the flat-bedded sandstones of the hills, which makes good walking, and, even when swamped with a foot of water, never causes mud. On the north and east, however, on slightly lower ground, these sandy ridges are less frequent; the villages, when possible, are built on them for health and convenience, while the paddy is grown below. The trails on these sides, passing chiefly through this low land, are in the rains two or three feet deep in thick, clinging mud.

If the houses of the Thai (in which for the moment we may include the Siamese and Laos together) are in the city badly situated in swamp and jungle, and badly kept in repair, the houses of the Chinese are very different; they are the flourishing part of the community. There are some thousands of them here and in the neighbourhood, nearly all shopkeepers, and outside the west gate, and along the main trail on each side, they have a regular village. The street is narrow between the open shop-fronts, and the road paved with baulks of timber. They drive a large trade among the people coming in from the distant parts, in calico stuffs, coloured sarongs and panungs, brasswork for betel boxes, trays, etc., umbrellas, sandals (the latter

 soles of leather with a strap coming up inside the great toe, and dividing and passing off on each side, which are used all over the north);

hats of straw, felt, or strips of palm leaf; bells for oxen, tins of Swiss milk, matches, needles and threads, wire and nails, cheap chains, a few tools of European type, coloured yarns, white jackets and singlets, towels, and even soap : all are imported from Bangkok. Yet, with the present difficulties of transport through the Dong Phya Yen, the Chinamen are doing a flourishing business.

The Chinese houses are peculiar ; a rectangular building being first built of large unbaked mud bricks, with pillars rising like chimneys at each end. Outside, several feet higher, and resting on these pillars, is constructed a *yah kah*, or grass roof. Big fires are kindled inside to dry the place; and the result is a very cool dwelling. The grass roofing is brought very often far out, overhanging the front, and this makes a shop front with the house behind.

These houses are usually on the roadsides, the two principal ones running north and south, and east and west, connecting the gates, and meeting about the centre. The latter road is about a mile long, the former less. The central market is carried on all day in a large roofed building near the centre of the city, and all up the road sit the yellow-faced Chinamen smoking their long-stemmed pipes in the shop fronts, and with the aid of their wives (generally Siamese, and good business women) bargaining with the long-haired, dark burned men from the plains, to whom the beauties of the shops in Khorat are a great delight. From these main roads one may have quite an extensive ride or walk without going outside the walls, in lovely lanes, lying deep down between high banks of shrubs and grasses (and sometimes 4 feet deep in water). These lanes are quite a feature of the country outside, too, and, with the long grassy slopes referred to above, would make Khorat the centre of delightful excursions in the cool months.

The journey from Khorat to Saraburi on the Nam Sak, whence Bangkok can be reached in two days, occupies as a rule six or seven days only. But when, after the main body had come up and had a day's rest, we bade good-bye to the unceasing kindness of the Commissioner, and at the end of the first day's march, which had begun pleasantly through lanes and villages, found ourselves up to our necks in water, it was evident we should take longer. We had to trend to the southward to get upon the high ground out of the water, and with constant delays, owing to the impassable state of the rivers, it was fourteen days before we got to Saraburi.

Leaving the beautiful villages outside Khorat, deep in their thick clusters of areca palms, which in places form perfect forests of tall stems supporting the arched roof of leaves far overhead, and making a perpetual cool shade, we had two days alternately over flat sandstone beds and flooded lowlands, where the water was for hours at a time up to our thighs, and at one place for half a mile up to our necks. Our nights were wretched, as the rain was perpetual, and the waggons could not arrive at the monasteries, where we put up, till long after midnight; the men lay sleeping round, hungry and damp, lots of them too tired to eat their supper when we got it ready, about 2 a.m.

These monasteries, built, as they were in days of old in our own Fen country, upon little islands, are often the only things above the vast surrounding lakes of water. The houses in the villages, built high on piles, keep dry. Raised above the ground some two or three feet, are generally long timber walks, made of solid felled trees, the top side being slightly shaved down, on which the monks may walk out dry and clean in the morning rounds to get their food. These walks are attached to the wats in all the plains of the country, and when the traveller strikes one, he knows a wat, with its welcome sala or resthouse, is near.

The trail follows the Khorat river to nearly its source in the limestones of the " Dong Phya Yen " forest; it then strikes across the forest, descending the spurs of the plateau to the elbow made by the Nam Sak, which turns away at Keng Koi in a west-south-westerly direction to the Meinam. This trail in the forest is greatly worn by the pack oxen, by which alone the thick forest can be penetrated, and in the rains is a series of narrow tracks winding in and out between the trees, consisting of frightfully slippery mud. The oxen have a way of walking in each other's footsteps, and the result is a series of ridges, like those on a sandbank at low water; but the ridges are greasy mud, and the depressions deep pitfalls. Thus in the wet weather the oxen constantly have heavy falls, and no one can get through without finding himself often on his nose or on his back.

The forest proper begins at Chanteuk, a small village, in the neighbourhood of which are some copper mines. These are open works, and as no one has worked there lately, were, when we passed through, brim full of water. On the Khorat side of this place are two fords, to cross which huge tree-trunks lie over the water, the growth along the bamboo being extraordinarily dense. Between them is a sala, which fortunately was in moderate condition, as we were delayed there two days in pouring rain, the river having risen ten feet in one night, as I measured next morning. Our quinine was nearly at an end; one man was quite prostrated with fever; and our eight days' store of rice was nearly done, all our chickens gone, the horses useless with sore backs, and the thirty-eight oxen carrying the packs suffering with coughs and sores. To get out we built two rafts; one was carried away on her first journey, the ropes going;

and the other proved so slow that, as the distance was some hundred yards in the then state of the water, it would have taken us two days to get all over. But, to our great satisfaction, the river fell.

At Chanteuk we got some rice and *platieng*, salt-fish, which the Siamese eat with their rice, and can live on for any length of time. Then, instead of going down the great trail, where a party of two men and a woman we met had just left two of their number dead of fever in the road, I took a drier, if longer route to the south. Our resting-places were Ban Kanong Pra, Ban Tachang, Hoay Sai, and Muak Lek Nua, whence we reached Keng Koi.

The scenery of this forest is most peculiar, and by no means inviting, especially in the continuous heavy rain, when the traveller is attacked by ticks and leeches, flies, and red ants seeking a dry place. The villages are the wretchedest collections of huts, the people mostly very poor; and one constantly wondered how any soul could live in these tiny clearings in the midst of a vast area where, for the most part, the sun never comes, when he might be in healthy, open country. We could seldom get even a banana. Undulating in all directions lies the forest, with now and then a sheet of limestone precipice towering among the drifting rains; the paths,* just wide enough for an ox, continually obstructed by lately fallen trees, round which a *detour* must be cut in the semi-darkness; and all the while the dull roar of the rain upon the leaves, with the prospect of a camp, wet through, in long six-feet grasses for the night. At Ban Mai we emerged from the forest, and found a clean village with a lot of cheerful, chatty Laos, who sent three men on with us to Keng Koi—the smartest set of men we had seen since leaving the Mekong.

At Pak Prio, a morning's walk beyond, we found the embankment of the railway to Khorat so far advanced as to have a mile of rails laid above the place, and a locomotive standing almost finished in a shed, to which my men as they came by fell upon their knees and offered the customary Siamese " salaam," by raising the clasped hands to the forehead. The oxen, which had reached a stream we crossed with ease a few hours before above Keng Koi, found it impassable, and were delayed two days there. My poor fellows, soaked through and through, and with no chance of getting snug at night, had to sleep and live for two days of pouring rain in the sala; but,

---

* There are a few elephant tracks.

being near home, were as jolly as could be. The temperature was some 4° higher at night, and mosquitos, which we had not seen for over five months, were most obnoxious; and from the strong south-west winds blowing, it was evident we were once more near the gulf.

One day's pulling and half a day's steaming, and Bangkok was in sight, with the French *Lutin* and H.M.S. *Swift* lying off the Legations. This was the first evidence we had had of there being political troubles. From fording the swollen streams, from continual tumbles in mud and water, and from constant rain, we found nearly everything on the pack oxen had been ruined that could be—photographs and other things. It is a most clumsy way of travelling, without doubt, and the time and labour spent in loading up every morning is enormous. The weights on the two sides must be adjusted accurately, the two men lifting them on a bamboo, through the middle, to test the balance and spending often ten minutes in getting one pair of panniers ready. Then there are constant falls, and often these are not discovered until miles have been traversed, and a careful search has to be made in ditches, streams, and mud for hours at a time. Besides this, the pace is wretchedly slow. This belt of the Dong Phya Yen, which can only be passed by animals, thus equipped, is a practical barrier to communication, leaving out of consideration the superstition with which the forest is, with much reason owing to its fevers, regarded, and the badness of the roads within it. The Khorat Railway becomes thus a work of the greatest importance to the whole plateau. To complete its usefulness, one or two passable cart-roads will do all that is necessary for that piece of undoubtedly hopeful country.

The Nam Sak, which the railway leaves at Keng Koi, is also a valuable river, inasmuch as, apart from the large tobacco crops towards its source, the valley is one richer in minerals than any other piece of country like it in Siam, and in the rainy season the question of transport is a fairly easy one. What struck me very much on descending the Nam Sak was the thickness of the population all along the banks, as compared with anything we had seen in the north. The beauty of the wats—always built on points of land round which the stream wound its turbid way—was also striking, and quite impressive. In the manners of the majority, and their loud talking, it was also clear that we were no longer among the gentle Laos of Nan or the musicians of Luang Prabang; but the comfort and luxury of the people were such as far exceeded anything we had seen since we left the Meinam at Pechai.

The weather all the way from Nongkhai to Muak Lek Nua (end of April and May) was south-westerly winds, moderate to fresh, falling at night. Mornings fine, with heavy cumuli in the south-west and west, which gradually spread, and became dark flashing thunder-clouds. Heavy rain after 2 p.m., beginning with a heavy squall of wind shifting to the west and north-west, and once or twice round to north-east, whence it blew hard for an hour. Rain generally lasted most of the night. Thermometer—average minimum reading, 70° Fahr.; maximum, 91° in the shade.

From Muak Lek Nua we descended into the Meinam valley, and found in the plains but slight showers, and fresh south-westerly wind lasting long into the night. Thermometer—minimum reading while in Pak Prio, 74°.

The result of so much wading made itself rather severely felt in a few days on most of us, and we had sores on our legs and feet for some time afterwards, so that it was almost impossible to get shoes on. This was no doubt partly owing to low diet, and partly to the cuts and wounds to the bare feet which every one gets wading where he cannot see his way, made worse by the blistering effect of the occasionally fierce sun, to keep off which palm leaves wrapt round the foot are excellent. With regard to the fevers, I would say, don't give quinine every day, as then in emergency its effect is less powerful, and the constitution is too accustomed to it; keep it until men feel a bit down, or when in very bad places or bad weather. It will last longer, and do more. In the high fevers of the dense forests, which prostrate a man very suddenly, emetics are the most reliable cure.

In a country abounding in snakes, it is not a little remarkable that our party only saw four the whole time. Again, though often in wild elephant tracks, none of us ever either saw or heard one. Two tigers, a few deer, and monkeys (which are not timid) were the only animals which were seen in the forests—a very sufficient proof, where their tracks are to be seen on every hand, and they can be heard around all night, of the care with which they avoid meeting man. Of course the great thickness of the vegetation, where the man in front of you is often out of sight even in the path, in great measure

H

also accounts for it, and it is this which prevents Siam being such a field for the sportsman as it would otherwise be.

There is one subject especially which it struck me often would make an interesting inquiry for any one who understands the subject— the comparison of the patterns and colours, both in the silk and cotton-work of the Laos districts ; such as the check patterns in the panungs and cloaks in Nan, the former remarkable for a large use of a bright yellow, which, to the unaccustomed eye is rather flaring, the latter for its red shades ; the horizontal and generally narrow stripes of the Luang Prabang petticoats (in which, again, the best effect is due to yellow) ; and the extremely taking panungs of Khorat, which are thought very much of by the Siamese. They are of one colour, with a border at the ends, blue, a delicate pink flesh colour, and a light red being the commonest.

Note on Gold and Silver at Luang Prabang.

All over the Laos states silver ornaments, as well as such articles as betel-boxes, trays, etc., are very common among the chiefs, and at Luang Prabang gold is likewise often seen used in place of silver for such things. The question is often raised as to how and where these metals have been obtained in such quantities in the past, that even tribute has been paid in ornaments made of them from olden times. Certainly the gold has always been found in alluvial sands, nor did I ever hear of its being known in veins or veags, nor did I ever find any traces of its so occurring. I believe its chief source must be the series of crystalline schists, which is an extensive one, and I incline to the idea, from the smallness of the quantities extracted from the sands, that it is probably sparsely disseminated through these rocks as well as through the quartz and possibly the calcareous veins, and that it will never be found in them in sufficient quantities to pay working. The patient streams have worked away for ages denuding and carrying away these rocks, and separating and depositing the gold, and all they have effected as far as the latter goes is that they have deposited infinitesimal quantities of it only, with larger quantities of the other minerals, such as magnetic iron ore, iron pyrites, etc. Decomposition and disintegration of the latter may be in places freeing more gold, and the yearly floods bring down their small addition, but yet even the Lao worker hardly finds it worth his while to work the sands, and the apathy displayed in the matter everywhere is partly without doubt accounted for by the poverty of the results obtained. And where the native worker gets such poor results, will the European miner get better ?

The gold in the Mekong is generally extremely fine and much water-worn, and is usually found below a sharp turn in the river, where the water runs strong. As regards the silver, it has been found native, but in such very small quantities that it cannot have supplied the whole country. The whole of Siam, however, is rich in galena, often of a very argentiferous character, and it may possibly have been found with other sulphides as well, but there can be little doubt that most of it has been extracted from galena. In some parts of the Northern Laos States this has been a regular industry. Small blast furnaces of baked mud are used, and when reduced the metal is run off in pigs and put in a reverberatory furnace with charcoal. This is sometimes done (but clumsily enough) further south, but little interest is manifested as a rule in these matters. Nowadays money is often melted down for working into ornaments.

APPENDIX.

AT the Meeting of the Royal Geographical Society on February 24, 1894, an account of Mr. Warington Smyth's journey by the President, Mr. Clements R. Markham, c.b., was read by Mr. Probyn. Before the reading of the paper, the President said—

The paper we are to hear this evening is on exploration on the Upper Mekong, in Siam, by Mr. Herbert Warington Smyth, who is serving under the Siamese Government. Siam is from many points of view a most interesting country, more particularly for us at the present time, and it is observable that until about nine years ago, when Mr. Holt Hallett read his paper, we had scarcely in this Society heard anything of Siam except as to the exploration of the Mekong by our gold medallist, Lieut. Garnier. We had only had scattered notices in previous years from Sir Robert Schomburgk and Sir Harry Parkes. But latterly we have received most important communications from Lord Lamington in 1891 and Mr. Curzon last year, and I think that not only this Society, but the nation generally, owes a debt of gratitude to Lord Lamington and Mr. Curzon for having so persistently, so patriotically, and so ably kept a question of such importance to England before the Government and the public. It was in 1887 that Mr. McCarthy, after surveying Siam for several years, favoured us with a most interesting communication. He was the first to describe to us the geographical and the general features of the country; and I believe I am right in saying it was through the advice and the persuasion of Mr. McCarthy that this young and modest explorer, Mr. Warington Smyth, was induced to send us his paper, which we shall listen to this evening.

Unfortunately, he will be unable to read it himself; he is still—I won't say better employed, because I don't think any one can be better employed than in reading a paper before this Society, but he is quite as well employed in preparing in Siam for further exploration, and I am glad to say that, as the paper is in manuscript, or the condensed version which we are obliged to use, a friend of Mr. Warington Smyth and an old schoolfellow, Mr. Probyn, has very kindly undertaken to read it.

After the reading of the paper, the following discussion took place:—

Lord LAMINGTON: I think I may say that if Mr. Warington Smyth had been here he would have considered it a great compliment to have had his lecture listened to by so large an audience, and I may also say you will not think your time wasted while listening to the paper. We owe a debt of gratitude to Mr. Probyn for having undertaken to read a paper so full of names to which he must be unaccustomed. With regard to the paper, no description I have read has recalled to me so vividly the scenes in that part of the world. Mr. Smyth has shown himself not only a geologist, but a close observer of natural history and human customs in every variety and form. He has represented to us most fully all the scenery, and given us a vivid description of Siamese and Laos life. I am glad that he corroborates what I myself would state, the gentleness of the Laos tribes. I don't know who has called them barbarians, but I cannot imagine a people less deserving of such a title. I am not quite sure of the definition of civilization, and in their own way it may not be Western, but in all kindness and honesty they are as worthy to be called civilized as any that could be found in the human race. I almost wish he had told us more about the mineralogical wealth of the country. I am not certain how far we may gather that the sapphire mines are of any great value, but from the mere fact of these Burmans coming over and thinking it worth while to take long journeys to sell their stones, and from their being of the first water, we may assume that when these mines are worked in a more efficacious manner they will prove to be of value. Another interesting part of his paper refers to the navigation of the Mekong from north of Luang Prabang and down south as far as Nong Khai. From Chieng Kong, where he first touched it, to Chieng Kan, we may assess its value as a navigable river, that is to say, for any boats of size to carry cargoes. His estimate is borne out by the report of Mr. Archer, and so also his statement on the commerce of Luang Prabang gives us a true idea of its worth, which is practically *nil*. Of course, we know the French are anxious to obtain possession of that place, as they consider it of first-class importance. Both Mr. Archer and Prince Henri d'Orleans think it, as a commercial centre, valueless for attracting any European capital. That part of the Mekong which may be considered navigable is from Chang Tang to Khong, further than Mr. Warington Smyth went. The French have now carried some stern-wheel steamers piecemeal up to these waters; the result of their enterprise only the future can show. With regard to the fishing methods of the natives, I may just say that these arrangements may be very well when you are descending the river, but they are the greatest inconvenience when ascending, as they form a formidable barrier if there is a strong current, and when you have to face this rigid fence of bamboos, it then becomes a matter of great difficulty to force the boat through.

Mr. Warington Smyth mentioned the difficulties made by the mud; this, of course, in the wet season renders all travelling impossible. The sliminess of the mud is almost inconceivable, and I can recollect, when between Chieng Upeng and Mung Sai, I used when climbing to keep on all fours, and probably slip down until arrested by a twist in the path; and it was amusing to see the efforts made by boys and men to mount the slimy slopes. This was in the dry season; in the wet season travelling with loaded animals becomes impossible throughout the greater part of the Indo-China peninsula. Mr. Archer came across from Chieng Kong into the Nam Nan valley; now Mr. Warington Smyth describes the country from Nong Khai to Khorat; and there is an account waiting to be published by Mr. Beckett, of the diplomatic service, of a journey still further down the Mekong and along the Nam Mun river to Khorat. We are thus in possession of descriptions of a country that, owing to political exigencies, will play an important part in the future, and all information we derive concerning it must be very valuable to us.

I apologize for addressing you at such length, and thank you for your kind remarks about my efforts to instruct public opinion about Siam. I imagine I must be a lineal descendant of Cassandra, because I have noticed that all I have said has been disregarded. I am glad to see Mr. Curzon has torn himself away from the charms of the allotment question. He has given much information, and has asked many searching questions in Parliament with reference to Siam, and has been successful in eliciting some valuable information.

Hon. GEORGE CURZON: Lord Lamington has indulged in some amiable chaff at the expense of the House of Commons, to which we are accustomed on the part of those noblemen who belong to the upper chamber. I may tell him, in reply, that what concerns us much more than the question of allotments for the parishes in England is the question of the future political allotment of Siam. My interest in Siam is more than a purely physical or geographical interest in the country; and all those who belong to the country, or have a friendly concern in it, may rest assured that neither Lord Lamington or I will abate any effort for its fair treatment in the politics of the future. I don't know that I have much right, perhaps none, to address you at all this evening, because, in the first place, I have not been upon these upper parts of the river Mekong which have been visited and so admirably described successively by Lord Lamington and in the paper this evening. My own acquaintance with the Mekong is limited to its lower portion, where it flows through Cochin-China, Cambodia, and at Priom Penh, the capital of Cambodia, sends northwards a branch that disembogues into the lake Tali Sap. Now, this Mekong river is one of the most remarkable rivers in the world, whether contemplated in the lower parts, where it spreads out in broad tranquil reaches from 200 yards to half a mile in width; or whether you examine its middle sections, where, as we have been told this evening, the French are finding furious and stormy rapids; or whether you go northward beyond the exploration of Lord Lamington and Mr. Warington Smyth, the river pursues its course unknown and unexplored far away, amid the mountain masses of Western China and Tibet. This river Mekong seems to me, during the last twenty-five years, to illustrate a lesson, ever since 1865-6, when the French expedition under Lagree, Garnier, and De la Porte went up the river to explore it,—one of the most heroic of expeditions in its conception and execution, and most pathetic in its result, undertaken by pioneers. Ever since then it has had an extraordinary fascination for Frenchmen—so much so, that they have claimed for themselves a sole right of interest in the Mekong, no matter what reports may be brought home by travellers, commercial agents, or explorers, as to the unnavigability of the river. They have maintained these ideas to the present day, and I cannot imagine a more interesting study than that of the parts which the great rivers of Asia, the Euphrates, Oxus, Ganges, and Mekong, have taken in history not merely by their geographical features or commercial aspect, but by what I may call their moral influences, exercised on the moulding of the peoples and on the destinies of empires. We have heard a most interesting paper from Mr. Smyth. He has given us a most faithful and vivid account of boat life, raft life, camp life, village life, and jungle life in Siam, and, as Lord Lamington said, has given us not only a faithful, but a singularly attractive, picture of the various tribes who inhabit that country. I was glad to hear what Lord Lamington said about these Laos peoples, because there is too great a tendency in the world to assume that, because the tribes of little-known and comparatively unexplored districts have not all the abominable manners of civilization, they must necessarily be described as barbarians. As he remarked, no more amiable, docile population exists—a people possessed of æsthetic and musical tastes, who are entitled to the epithet, "the Greeks of the Indo-Chinese peninsula." There is another strip south of Luang

Prabang, right down between the mountains and the Mekong, into which no Englishman has ever been; and, looking to the fact that the French have taken possession of it, I don't suppose we are likely to go there. Further down is a curious people called Ladans, amongst whom an adventurer, either French or Italian, established himself a short time ago, called himself king, and, I believe, wanted to appear in the " Almanack de Gotha ; " but, having retired for a short time, on his return found his subjects unwilling to receive him, and the kingdom has disappeared. The interest to us in this room is not that of acquisition or conquest, but a friendly sympathetic interest in the Oriental people who are playing their own part in the world, in proportion as they come into the mesh of British trade. I was interested to hear about Manchester goods at Luang Prabang, seeing the advantages the French have for shipping by Hanoi and up the Black river. You would never expect Manchester goods there, and the fact that they are there means, not only that they ought to be kept there, but ought to be seen all over the peninsula. I am pleased to say that Mr. Smyth, in the latter part of his journey, travelled over a line that is to be taken by the railway from Khorat to Bangkok, of which I saw the embankments. It was largely the anticipation of the results of that railway that induced the French to go on, for the flow of trade has been for some time past from the Mekong river south-westwards. They want to divest it towards their possessions. Conceive how it will be emphasized if you have a railway instead of the carts that take goods laboriously by the way Mr. Smyth described ! I am sorry that there is difficulty about this railway—that the contractor has had a dispute with the Siamese Government; but I hope that this will be settled, and, at all events, that Siam will make the railway. A year ago I was in Siam, and the king told me he meant to take the railway to Kong Khai. It will be the best thing for the salvation of his country, and there is no Englishman present who does not wish to see Siam strong, independent, and wealthy, and capable of holding its own. For my own part, I shall never cease to feel the greatest and warmest interest in that singularly attractive country, and my own opinion is, that it is the duty of every British Government to see that the integrity of that country is not wiped out, and that its vitality is maintained.

Mr. F. VERNEY: I have the honour of being connected with Siam by being a member of the Siamese legation. I have watched with intense interest the advance of that country, and have been concerned in its connection with Europe even more than with Siam itself. I can thoroughly confirm everything that has been said by Lord Lamington on the one side and Mr. Curzon on the other, from what I have heard, not from what I have seen. I was in Siam for a very short time, and was treated there with the greatest possible kindness and hospitality. To judge fairly the civilization of that country, we should take, not our own standard of civilization only, but a wider standard applicable to communities differing entirely in their origin, their histories, and in their development from our own, and it is very gratifying to hear a man in Mr. Curzon's position in the House of Commons express his opinions in the emphatic and eloquent language to which we have just listened. It is true that only recently England has awakened to the extreme importance of that distant country. It was not until the other day that Englishmen had an idea that Siam produced anything much besides twins, but this cynical ignorance is rapidly disappearing. You cannot listen to travellers like Lord Lamington and Mr. Curzon (and when Mr. Warington Smyth comes back we shall listen to him) without finding out that there is a great deal both of material and what we may call moral progress in that distant country. Let me say one word as regards his Majesty the King of Siam, on whose character and personality so much depends. For many years past the king has been known as a man of wide interests, of a very high order of intelligence, and of an unusual charm of manner. He comes of a family distinguished in the past both for statesmanship and scientific culture. A member of his family was one of the greatest astronomers in the East; another was described to me by one of the greatest Oriental travellers, and perhaps the most cultivated linguist in Germany, as being the master of more languages than any other man he had met; and you may be assured that the royal family of Siam will produce many more distinguished men. There are members studying at Oxford, others at our public schools, growing up surrounded by all the best English influences. Let us hope that Siam and England will go hand-in-hand, and that other countries in Europe will come round to see that this is not a country for invasion or annexation, but worthy of support and sympathy, on account of its people, its products, its achievements in the past, and its possibilities for the future.

Mr. Louis: I am afraid I can add very little to what Mr. Warington Smyth has said, because my explorations were in a diametrically opposite direction. I had the pleasure of his company when exploring some diamond and ruby mines in the south-east, and this was more interesting to me as my knowledge of mineralogy was acquired under Mr. Warington Smyth's father. On one point only I have to differ from Mr. Warington Smyth—as to the Burmese way of washing rubies and sapphires. It is not at all to my mind the crude, rough way he mentions. Their baskets are the most beautifully finished work made of bamboo in thin strips, and handled with all the deftness and practised skill of an Australian or Californian gold-washer; they scarcely ever miss a gem, so far as I could see, much bigger than a pin's head. As regards the geology of these districts on the east of Chantabun, the formation is simply gravel from 2 to 5 feet deep overlying the trap rocks, and these gems have been worn out of the trap rocks by natural agencies. Mr. Smyth describes the gems as coming from a black crystalline rock very similar to that I have mentioned. This formation seems to be quite different from the white limestone occurring in Burma. I should like to mention one thing that must have struck very few when hearing Mr. Smyth's paper; it not only gives a wonderfully accurate description of the people, but is an accurate reflex of his own plucky and cheery nature; very few can have any idea of the real hardships and difficulties and dangers involved in such an expedition. It takes an Englishman to go through such dangers and hardships, and then write such a bright account of everything as Mr. Smyth has done.

The President: I am sure the meeting will agree with me that we have never in this hall heard so graphic and so picturesque an account of this little-known region as is contained in Mr. Warington Smyth's paper. Mr. Smyth is evidently a keen observer of nature, and has the gift of sympathy—of being able to place himself in the position of the people with whom he travels and whom he comes across, as well as a kindly feeling for the animals serving with him. These are very high qualities. His narrative is so lively and cheery, that we can hardly realize the amount of hardship and danger the journey entailed. These are all admirable qualifications, which are due almost entirely, I have no doubt, to his own individuality; but perhaps we may put something down to his education. Mr. Warington Smyth was a Westminster boy, like his father before him, who was a valued member of our Council. I cannot help taking this opportunity of saying that there are very few places of learning in this country that have done in times past so much for geography as that glorious old school which nestles round the cloisters of Westminster Abbey. Richard Hakluyt, the father of English Geography, was a Westminster boy; Edmund Gunter, the first introducers of the use of Napier's logarithms; Neville Maskelyne, to whom we owe the Nautical Almanac; Dr. Vincent, one of our greatest comparative geographers, were all Westminster boys; and one of the seven founders of this Society, and two of your Presidents, were also Westminster boys. Now we find a Westminster boy training himself, hereafter to be a great explorer, and perhaps discoverer. Let us wish him all success in his career, and I am sure the meeting will desire me to convey to him a hearty and unanimous vote of thanks.

INDEX.

A.

ADJUTANTS or *nok karien* of the Mekong district, 67

Archer, Mr., journey in Siam, 102

B.

BAN BAR, 76
—— Bodibun, 87
—— Mai, 95
—— Nam Pi, iron mines at, 14
—— Satan, 35
—— Soap Ta or Pak Ta, 46
—— Ton Kluay, 34
—— Tum, 87
Banana trees, wild, 31
Bangkok to Muang Nan, route from, 1
Bells of wood in the wats, 78, 79
Birds and fish of the Siamese rivers, 7
Birds of the Mekong, 66
Boat-travelling in Siam and China, 1
Boria, Wat, 12
Buddha, statues of, 11, 12
Buffaloes of Siam, 85
Burmese gem-digging, 37, 38
——————— houses, 39
——————— method of washing rubies, 105

C.

CHANTEUK, copper mines near, 94
Cherim, road to, 15
Chieng Kan, 71
——————— Koug, 36, 37
——————— and Chieng Klan, 24
——————— district, temperature of the, 40
——————— to Luang Prabang, voyage from, 43
Chieng Tong, Wat, 56
Chinareth, Wat, 10, 11
Chinese boat-travelling, 1

Chinese houses and trade at Khorat, 92, 93
Chow Muang, funeral ceremonies of the, 39
Chulabut, 87
Cormorants of the Mekong, 66
Curzon, Hon. G., remarks on Mr. Warington Smyth's journey, 103

D.

DOI LUANG range, 53 *note*
Doug Choi, 30
——— Phya Yon forest, 94–96

E.

EAGLES of the Mekong district, 67
Elephant travelling on the Upper Mekong, 42
Elephants in Siam, 16

F.

FA PA rapids, 41
Fevers in travelling in Siam, 97
Fishing stakes and shelters on the Nam Oo, 65
French commerce at Luang Prabang, 57, 58
——— on the Mekong, 103, 104
Funeral ceremonies of the Chow Muang, 39

G.

GEM-DIGGING in neighbourhood of Nam Ngau, 36, 37
Geology of districts east of Chantabun, 105
Gold and silver at Luang Prabang, Note on, 98
——— washings on the Nam Ngau, 43, 44

THE CENTRAL PART OF
THE KINGDOM OF SIAM.
Showing the route of Mr. H. Warington Smyth.
1892-1893.
Heights in feet.
Scale of Miles.
One inch = 44 miles
Route

Explanation of Siamese Terms.
B. Ban, House, village   M. Me, ... River.
Chieng Muong, Governor   M. Muang, Town, Township
Do.Doi, Mountain.   N. Nam, ... River.
H. Houy, Stream.   N. Nong, ... Swamp
N. Nan, Hill.   P. Pak, Mouth of River.
Kh. Klong, Stream, Canal   P. Phen, ... Mountain
K. Kong, Rapid.   S. Sala, ... Rest House
L. Luang, Grave, Chief.   W. Wat, ... Monastery.

Angle and direction of dip of rocks
Gold, Sapphires, Copper
Lead, Iron.

www.ingramcontent.com/pod-product-compliance
Lightning Source LLC
Chambersburg PA
CBHW022141020726
47496CB00008B/2492